God, The Devil, And The Perfect Pizza

God, The Devil, And The Perfect Pizza

TEN PHILOSOPHICAL QUESTIONS

Trudy Govier

broadview press

Canadian Cataloguing in Publication Data

Govier, Trudy
    God, The Devil, And The Perfect Pizza

ISBN 0-921149-50-6

1. Philosophy. I. Title

          B72.G68 1989   100   C89-095126-8

broadview press
P.O. Box 1243
Peterborough, Ontario
K9J 7H5   Canada

in the U.S. broadview press
421 Center St.
Lewiston, NY
14092   USA

TABLE OF CONTENTS

PREFACE

These dialogues and stories express my affection for the apparently imponderable questions of philosophy and my conviction that it can be both enlightening and entertaining to think about them.

Conversations with my husband Anton Colijn and our daughter Caroline were a major source of inspiration for a number of the selections here. I've also benefitted from the comments and encouragement of Helen Hooker, Bette Strang, Renate Weber, Mark Weinstein, and reviewers for Broadview Press.

Illustrations are done by Calgary freelance artist Ian Doig.

Trudy Govier.

CAN COMPUTERS CHEAT?

Jan: How do you like the new computer game?

Robin: It's pretty good, but I'm not winning as much as I should. Well, I shouldn't complain—at least it doesn't cheat. Shelley's computer starts to cheat her when she's won a few games in a row. Does she ever get mad!

Jan: What do you mean, it cheats?

Robin: It doesn't play fair. Shelley does everything right and then, just when she's about to win the game, her player falls down dead on the screen, for absolutely no reason. She loses even after making all the right moves, and does she get frustrated! The darn computer cheats!

Jan: Come on, get serious. Computers can't cheat. They aren't people—they're only machines.

Robin: Well, Shelley has played a lot of games with that computer of hers, and she sure thinks it can cheat.

Jan: What does it take to cheat?

Robin: You mean what do you have to do to cheat? You have to break the rules and try to win the game in some way that's against the rules.

Jan: OK, and there's more than that. If you do win after breaking the rules, you still have to pretend you won by playing fair.

1

Robin: I don't quite get you.

Jan: Well, suppose you cheated on a test.

Robin: I never do.

Jan: All right, all right. But suppose you did. When you write a test, you are supposed to answer from your own knowledge. Somebody who cheats on an exam breaks this rule, because he puts down answers based on somebody else's knowledge. That's not all, though. To cheat, he has to try to fool the teacher into thinking that his answers came from his own head. Cheating is breaking the rules, but it's more than that. It's trying to get a better result than you could if you followed them, and pretending afterwards that you got your result by doing things the proper way.

Robin: What a mouthful! So, all right, cheaters are smarter than we think. Still, so what? Shelley's computer can cheat. When her man gets zapped just at the climax of the game, for no reason, the computer is breaking the rules. I can tell you, this sort of behavior gets on your nerves when you're all wound up in one of these games.

Jan: Too bad. Poor Shelley. But still, whatever she thinks, her computer isn't cheating. To cheat, you have to know the rules and deliberately break them to try to get a better result. You also deceive other people, making them think you got your result the right way. Computers can't do all this. They don't know rules, they can't aim at results, and they can't pretend. Therefore they can't cheat. Period. It's an unanswerable argument.

Robin: Some unanswerable arguments can be answered
          then, I guess. Look, it's a matter of what com-
          puters do. We play games with them. They seem
          for all the world as if they're cheating. It looks like
          cheating, it feels like cheating, it *is* cheating. If
          Shelley can't tell the difference between what her
          computer does and cheating, then isn't it cheat-
          ing?

Jan: I'm telling you, to cheat you have to know the
          rules. Computers don't know the rules, so they
          don't cheat.

Robin: Look, computers usually do play games according

to the rules. They must know the rules, or they couldn't do this.

Jan: Computers know rules? Come on, computers are just so much fancy hardware. They don't know rules, and they don't know anything else either.

Robin: Well, they *quotes* know rules. You know what I mean. The rules have got to be in there somehow, or else the computer couldn't play the game at all.

Jan: What do you mean?

Robin: If a computer is playing a game, it's because somebody wrote the software for it. That means somebody wrote a program that tells it what to do in the game. Stuff like, 'in this circumstance, do this; in that circumstance, do that'. Of course the program would use computer symbols, probably, not just English words. But the game has rules and those rules are used when the program is made up. If they weren't, then the computer couldn't play the game. It *is* operating according to the rules — most of the time.

Jan: Except when it cheats?

Robin: Right. Except when it cheats.

Jan: So it operates according to the rules because it has a program, and the programmer knew the rules and used them when he wrote the program. But that doesn't show the *computer* knows the rules. Or even that it *quotes* knows the rules — whatever you mean by that.

Robin: The computer is programmed to play by the rules and it can play by the rules. It must know the rules, or how could it do this? How could it possibly behave just as if it knows the rules, if it doesn't know the rules? It doesn't make sense.

Jan: It's programmed; it's not that it knows anything. What the computer does isn't based on any thought or understanding, because it's only programmed. Just because it seems most of the time to be following rules, that doesn't mean there is anything like knowledge inside. Computers are machines, not conscious beings. They can't gather evidence, think about choices, consider rules in order to apply them, compare rules of one game to rules of another, or any of that. For heaven's sake, computers aren't people!

Robin: But people aren't the only creatures who know things. Animals do, and God too, if there is a god. If there are Martians, they might know things. You can't say that just because computers aren't people, they have no knowledge. It's blind prejudice.

Jan: Well, all right. You can't *define* knowledge as only for people, I'll grant you that. But all the other things you mention would be conscious, and would be able to learn from experience, and make decisions. Computers can't do that because they can't have thoughts. There is no thought inside a computer and there is no consciousness, because the computer is only a machine. It's not a thinking thing and there's nothing going on inside.

Robin: What do you mean, nothing goes on inside a computer? Where have you been? Millions of things are going on inside. That's what hardware and software are all about.

Jan: The hardware is chips and wires and metal and so on, and the software is programs made up by people, making the hardware work in a certain way. But there aren't any thoughts and there's no attention. Computers don't think about what they're doing when they play according to rules. They aren't aware of rules the way people are, so you can't say they know the rules.

Robin: That's too simple, if you ask me. Computers act as though they follow the rules and they are programmed according to the rules, so you might as well say they know the rules. So what if their insides are metal and wires and so on, instead of blood and cells and bones? What difference does that make, if the question is whether they know the rules?

Jan: To know something you have to understand it and believe it and have evidence or reasons. If knowledge were just behavior, we'd have to say all kinds of machines know things. Thermostats, even, or toasters. Does a toaster know the rules for turning white toast into bread? After all, a toaster is based on rules, or you could say so. When bread is put in and a side button is pushed, toast comes out a few minutes later. But that doesn't show the toaster knows anything!

Robin: That's not fair. Toasters are simple machines, not complicated ones like computers. It's not right to compare a toaster and a computer. There is some sense in which a computer *does* know rules, even if its knowledge is nothing like human knowledge.

Jan: I can't believe you're not convinced! It seems so obvious to me that what happens inside a computer isn't enough for knowledge. But anyway, to get back to the idea of cheating, even if we say that computers *in some sense* know the rules, that doesn't show they can cheat. To cheat, a computer would not only have to know the rules and deliberately break them, it would have to pretend to have followed the rules. Isn't that a bit fancy for a machine?

Robin: Computers are fancy machines — real fancy.

Jan: Do you really think a computer is trying to win when it plays a game?

Robin: Of course. If it weren't, it wouldn't play so well, and the games wouldn't be fun for Shelley and me.

Jan: It's trying, really trying, to win? Come on, you can't mean it.

Robin: Sure. It makes sense. You just have to think about it a bit. The program is written to give the computer a decent chance of winning the game. It requires certain moves in certain circumstances, and the purpose of these moves is to let it win the game. The program is organized around this goal. The computer is programmed around winning. Therefore when it plays the game, it's trying to win.

Jan: Therefore?

Robin: Yeah, therefore.

Jan: That's quite a logical jump! You can't say that just because the program was written by the programmer for the purpose of getting the machine to win, the computer itself is trying to win. It just doesn't follow!

Robin: Sure it does. It's programmed to play to win. It sure acts like it's trying to win. So in a sense it's trying to win.

Jan: OK, so now we are getting another special *sense* for these words. *In a sense,* the computer knows the rules, because its responses are based on a program and the program is based on those rules. *In a sense* it is trying to win, because its program is written with the goal of winning in mind. But this *in a sense* stuff can be tricky.

Robin: How do you mean?

Jan: Think about it. *In a sense* I'm just as smart as Einstein. Yeah, in this sense: if Einstein were me, he'd have the very same ideas I do. By the way, Einstein was obviously a genius, so you should be convinced by my arguments!

Robin: Let's keep Einstein out of it. He gets enough corny publicity. It must make him turn right over in his grave!

Jan: The thing is, you are only keeping up your side of the argument by all this "in a sense" stuff. You just keep watering down all the important words and making them mean something else when they apply to computers. It makes the whole question so slippery! It's really starting to bother me.

Robin: Don't be so picky. I'm interested in computers and what they can do, not in sitting around arguing about words. That's boring.

Jan: So what about the business of deception and

pretense? A person who cheats on an exam has to pretend that his answers were arrived at by following the rules. But can computers pretend? Of course not. It just doesn't make sense.

Robin: It's not so complicated to pretend you get answers in the right way when you cheat on a test. You just hand in the exam, look the teacher straight in the eye, and leave the room. Not that I'd ever do it, of course. But it doesn't require a whole lot of fancy conscious gymnastics inside the mind or brain. For a computer to pretend to have beaten Shelley by following the rules is nothing special. It just means it doesn't show it broke the rules by squeaking, flashing lights, breaking down, or anything.

Jan: And *that's* all it means to have pretended to follow the rules? If that's all it takes to pretend, maybe the world is full of machines, all pretending all the time, and we don't even know it. This could really drive you crazy!

Robin: Maybe. Who knows? But for most machines there's no reason to think they're cheating. I'm not nuts, you know. I don't go around imagining that my toaster and my vacuum and my car are all having secret thoughts and trying to deceive me. But Shelley's computer is something else, because it does act as if it's cheating when it's playing that game. Toasters and vacuums and cars don't act as if they're cheating. That's the whole point.

Jan: Acting as if it's cheating and cheating aren't the same thing though, are they? Just because you and Shelley feel as though it's cheating, that doesn't mean it is. Have you ever heard of the Turing

Test?

Robin: No. What's that?

Jan: It's this idea from the forties, before there were
          many computers. Lots of people believe it today,
          but I think it's really silly.

Robin: So what is it?

Jan: Turing tried to describe what would have to hap-
          pen before it would be right to say that computers
          think. You'd have to have a situation where you
          put a person with one printer and a computer with
          another printer. Then a judge, in a different room,
          would be connected up with these printers, and
          would send questions and get back printed
          answers. If this judge receiving the print-out
          couldn't tell the person's responses from the
          computer's responses, then the computer would
          be responding just as intelligently as the person,
          so far as the judge could tell. Then, Turing said, it
          would make sense to say the computer could think.
          That was more or less it, I think. They call it the
          Turing Test. If a computer could pass this test, it
          would think.

Robin: Well that sounds sensible. Great! What's so
          wrong about the Turing Test?

Jan: You can see why it's wrong if you think about using
          the test for another purpose. It's just too simple-
          minded. Turing himself made a great comparison
          between this game — I think he called it the Imita-
          tion Game — and a similar test you might do using
          a man and a woman.

Robin: To see if you could tell the man from the woman,

from what they typed out? They're trying to fool the judge, and they have to respond to his questions by typing out answers on printers?

Jan: Right. They're trying to fool the judge. Otherwise the test wouldn't make sense, right? The judge could just ask, "are you a woman?" and it would type out yes or no.

Robin: So what's so silly about this?

Jan: Think about it. If someone couldn't tell a man from a woman using this test, that wouldn't prove there was no difference between men and women. It would just prove the judge made a mistake — probably because the kind of evidence he could get in such a crazy situation is too limited to matter in the first place. If he could give them a medical, he'd obviously know.

Robin: Would it prove men and women *think* the same way, even if they obviously aren't the same in other ways? After all, the thing with computers and people is about thinking.

Jan: I don't think it really proves anything. The situation is so unreal. And anyway, the person doing the experiment might just be wrong — I mean, maybe he can't find differences, even though they are really there. That's what you're ignoring with this cheating thing. Sure, maybe the behavior seems to Shelley and you just like cheating. But to cheat, her computer would have to be aware of what it's doing and trying to deceive her. It just doesn't do this. Just because Shelley thinks the computer is cheating when her man falls down dead, that doesn't mean the machine is really

11

trying to trick her.

Robin: Well, if the machine's not cheating, then what does go wrong?

Jan: What must be happening is that the program is weird in some way. Either that, or her machine just breaks down sometimes.

Robin: Well, maybe it's better to say that it cheats, but in a different way from the way people do, since it isn't conscious and can't be aware of what it's doing.

Jan: Machines cheat, but in a *special sense*? Not this again!

Robin: When computers cheat, they work outside the normal rules of the game, and what they do seems to us like cheating. You know, when I see Shelley playing that game with her computer and she's just about got it, and is on the verge of winning, and then the player falls over dead for no reason, then *that* looks like the machine is cheating.

Jan: Maybe. But it isn't cheating, since cheating requires deliberately breaking the rules, and trying to win, and pretense. You agreed computers can't cheat in that sense, and that is what cheating is. So how can you turn around now and insist that computers cheat after all! For once and for all, looking to somebody like cheating is not the very same as cheating. I don't care what Turing said, behavior isn't everything, and judges can make mistakes.

Robin: Computers do something that looks to us like cheating and feels to us like cheating when we're playing games with them. So we call it cheating. So what? It's just a matter of a word having two meanings. You know, like "squash." It can be either a game or a vegetable.

Jan: It can be an action verb too, like when you squash a juice box and it pops. I keep trying to squash your arguments, but I don't think I'm getting anywhere.

Robin: Squashing arguments is just as peculiar as a computer cheating.

Jan: It's obviously just a way of talking. A metaphor, you know. I don't really mean an argument can be squashed the way a juice box can.

Robin: But you assumed I could understand you when you said "squash an argument." And I can. If lots of people talked that way, we could say that the word "squash" is getting a new meaning. It would then have four separate meanings instead of three. I don't see what would be so bad about that. Lots of us say computers cheat, so soon "cheat" will have a new meaning that describes what they do.

Jan: Sure, sure, victory by definition. You can define the word in your own new way, and then insist that computers cheat. Maybe I'll just define "squash" in my own new way and insist that I've squashed your arguments.

Robin: But it's *not* just my definition. Lots of people think of their computers as knowing rules, thinking, trying — even cheating. They talk about computer knowledge and memory and computers searching for things, and stuff like that. And there are lots of other new things too. Like these computer viruses you hear about, the ones that get into a system of programs and destroy it. Viruses attack living things, but people talk about computer viruses and when they do, it doesn't make them think computers are alive or anything. Language just adapts and changes, whether you like it or not.

Jan: Well, you have a point. But I don't like it. I think all these ways of thinking and talking make computers seem too much like people. Computers *aren't* people. They're just machines!

Robin: People aren't as silly as you seem to think. They know the difference between machines and other people. They don't expect computers to taste ice cream and pizza or enjoy music or fall in love or feel the spring breeze. For heaven's sake! People aren't completely stupid. They don't think computers are going to get a fever because there is a computer virus around, and just because they talk about computer memory, they don't think computers sit around gabbing about the past.

Jan: I wouldn't be so sure. Have you ever known a real hacker? You know, one of those guys who spends about fifteen or sixteen hours a day working with his computer? You should try talking to a hacker some time. They talk about computers as though they were real people. They get so carried away working on them, they can hardly relate to any normal human being.

Robin: That does sound pretty weird. Do they call the computer "he" or "she"?

Jan: Always "he".

14

Robin: Gee, that's odd. I wonder why.

Jan: I don't know. Maybe they think computers reason and do math and logic, and those are male activities. It's funny because when men talk about cars and ships and so on, they usually call them "she".

Robin: Well, it doesn't mean anything, I guess.

Jan: It suggests a kind of attitude, though, doesn't it? Maybe the car is a *she* because the man drives it, whereas the computer is a *he* because he relates to it as an equal.

Robin: Good grief! You really take things too seriously. Normal people aren't like hackers, and they understand perfectly well that a computer is not a person and you don't have the kind of relationship with a computer that you have with a person.

Jan: Still, I wish we didn't use all these human mind words for computers. It really bothers me. I wish we didn't talk about computer memory, for instance. At one time the British talked about computer stores instead of computer memory. They just wanted a word to express the idea that a lot of information was stored in the computer, so they used "computer store". It seems perfectly sensible, not misleading.

Robin: OK, but you don't hear that expression much any more. Obviously people preferred talking about computer memory, because that's what we hear about now.

Jan: That's true, but it wasn't so much a matter of what people liked. The way I heard the story, the

Americans used "memory", and the British used "store". Then, because the Americans tended to make more computers and better ones than the British, it was their word that caught on.

Robin: All right, so people didn't exactly choose the word. But still, they accepted it. And more and more, words like "knowledge" and "memory" are used for computers, whether picky people like you like it or not. Of course computers aren't just like people and they don't make choices and decisions and pay attention and all that. But they do have knowledge and memory. Haven't you heard of artificial intelligence? There are lots of experts who think that computers will be able to think some day. In fact, some of them even think they're doing it already.

Jan: That just shows how confused you can get. People know perfectly well that computers do what they do because of the way they are programmed. Because they get fancy results, we may get the impression that they can do things like remembering and cheating. We get these bad habits of language and we can't think clearly any more.

Robin: That's ridiculous.

Jan: I really mean it. If we think about it clearly, artificial intelligence just doesn't make sense.

Robin: What about artificial stupidity? Could you have that?

Jan: Come on, Robin. Don't bug me. Look, computers aren't intelligent beings. They are fancy complicated machines and they can give us marvellous results. But they don't think, calculate, pay attention, deliberate, follow rules, pretend, cheat, or anything like it.

Robin: I don't think it's quite so simple.

Jan: Look, suppose we really thought computers were intelligent beings. We'd have to make them legal persons and give them the right to vote, wages, holiday pay, and all that. Computers would have to have civil rights and be protected by anti-discrimination laws and stuff. Wouldn't that be ridiculous? The point is, computers are machines we can use as we wish. They don't have thoughts and feelings, and if they did, we couldn't use them anymore, not the way we do, anyhow. It would be really immoral.

Robin: There's no point arguing about whether it's good or bad to use words like "artificial intelligence," "computer memory," "computer knowledge," and so on, is there? I mean people already do use these expressions and we couldn't stop them if we wanted to.

Jan: We couldn't. But tell me, after all this, *does* the computer cheat when it plays with Shelley?

Robin: Not really. Well, not the way people cheat anyway.

Jan: If there is any cheating, it's the programmer who cheats. One of those hackers, maybe, who has had his conscience warped by spending all his time with computers instead of people. Shelley's computer must be operating according to some program that explains what it does when she's playing that game.

Robin: How do you mean?

Jan: Well, if it makes her man fall down dead when she is about to win, this can only be because it is programmed to do that. Right?

Robin: Either that or it has broken down.

Jan: OK, but it hasn't broken down, because she can play the same game or other games right away afterwards, and things work fine.

Robin: That's right. Also it would be too much coincidence for the machine to break down again and again just at the same point in the game.

Jan: The computer must be programmed to sometimes wipe out her man, just when she's about to win. It has a program that makes us think it's cheating.

Robin: Not all the time, though. Quite often Shelley wins. The program doesn't always make the machine knock her man down at the end, only sometimes. It must be a pretty tricky program, eh?

Jan: It must be programmed: sometimes default at stage such-and-such. Or however you'd say that in the computer language, I don't know. So if anyone cheats it's the programmer, who put that instruction in.

Robin: Right. Computers don't cheat. They're too honest.

Jan: Oh groan! You'll never learn.

THE SPERM, THE WORM, AND FREE WILL

Robin: That business about computers cheating — you know, there was one argument you could have used to prove computers can't cheat. I don't know why you didn't think of it.

Jan: What?

Robin: Cheating is immoral — it's wrong — and to do something wrong, you have to have free will. Since computers don't have free will, they can't cheat.

Jan: So now you're convinced?

Robin: I'm still not sure. But why didn't you use the argument about free will?

Jan: I did think of it. But I'm not so sure about free will, actually. I don't know who has it, or even what it is, really.

Chris: You always hear about people doing things of their own free will, so some people at least must think they understand what it is.

Robin: I read the strangest report the other day, in a science magazine. It was called "The Existential Decision of a Sperm." The author seemed to think that even sperm had free will.

Chris: Good grief! Even computers would have a better

chance of having free will than sperm, I think. What on earth did he mean?

Robin: Well, what I read was just a report about another article, but apparently this scientist had described the life of a sea urchin, right from its first beginnings. He said the sea urchin sperm had three profound decisions to make. The most profound, and the first, was whether it should combine with a sea urchin egg to make a new being or whether it should go on existing separately.

Jan: But Robin, sperm don't have any brains and they certainly don't think, so how could they make decisions? The scientist was just probably trying to make his ideas sound exciting so more people would read his article. You don't really think he believed that sperm make decisions, do you?

Robin: I guess not, but you'd never know it from the way the report was written, saying things like "the sperm must ask itself" and "once the sperm decides." Boy, if a sperm can make an existential decision and have free will, anything can!

Chris: Once upon a time a human sperm made a free decision, and the result was you, Robin.

Robin: Ha ha. Anyway, if the sperm had to make a free decision, the ovum would too. It would have to decide not to fight the sperm off.

Chris: I wonder whether worms have free will.

Jan: Worms? Why ask?

Chris: Well, they are pretty simple creatures, but at least they have a primitive brain, so it is barely possible they might make decisions. It makes more sense than the idea of sperm having free will.

Robin: I never really watched worms closely enough to know.

Jan: All I know is 'the early bird gets the worm'. Presumably worms don't have much free choice then!

Chris: Well let's follow up on that one. The reason early birds are supposed to get the worm is that it's moist in the early morning and the worms come up from the earth to the surface and lie in the grass. You see the same thing when it rains a lot. There are worms all over the place, even on the sidewalks.

Robin: So what does this have to do with whether worms have free will?

Chris: I'm trying to imagine when a worm might have to make a choice, if that would make any sense at all. Imagine a worm being underground at, say, 5 in the morning. Suppose it has to choose whether to come up. If it chooses to come up to the surface, has it decided to do something? Does it have free will?

Jan: I don't know. I mean, isn't there something in worms that just makes them come up when it's wet? Instinct, or reflexes, or something?

Chris: If it were that simple, then they'd all be on the surface because in all of them instincts or reflexes would work the same way. But there are some still in the ground: some come up and some don't. So I guess it's more than an inborn instinct or reflex.

Jan: But even so, that wouldn't show that the worms that do come up have made a choice! I mean, just because we don't know whether a particular worm is going to surface or not, that doesn't mean the worm is making its own decision about it. Choice and free will don't come to the worm merely because we don't know about it.

Robin: Oh, I see what you're getting at. It's like watching a beautiful golden poplar tree on a fall day. Leaves are drifting down off the tree, and you can sit by the window watching them. You know that many, not all, will fall to the ground that day. Still, if you sit looking at one leaf in particular, you almost never know whether it will fall or not. It's not because the leaf can choose, it's just because you can't tell how loosely it's attached and you don't know how hard the wind will hit that branch. There certainly isn't anything like choice or free will. Actually, now that I think about it, it would be silly to think that worms have free will—just about as silly as thinking that sperm have it.

Jan: Why?

Robin: Worms can't think.

Chris: Their brains don't have billions of neurons the way human brains do.

Jan: Do you think their brains are too simple for them to make choices and have free will?

Chris: Yeah. It just wouldn't be possible.

Robin: But what's interesting isn't whether sperm, or worms, or even computers have free will. The important thing is free will in people. That's what

I want to talk about. If we keep going at this worm's pace, we are never going to get off the ground.

Chris: Clever, clever.

Robin: About the brain, Chris, you seem to think that very simple brains couldn't give a creature any ability to make choices, whereas more complicated brains could. Is that right? There is no will in a simple primitive brain?

Chris: I think you need a pretty complicated brain. To make a choice, we have to think of at least two possible things we could do. We think of different things we could do, and then we pick one and act on it. That might take language. For sure it takes an ability to be aware of a situation where we can do something, and the different possible things we can do, and consequences and so on. Lots of things — I guess choice is pretty complicated. But I don't think there is a thing called the will which is inside complex brains and left out of primitive brains.

Robin: You don't? But we all have free will! Our will must be something inside us.

Jan: Think of it this way, Robin. Suppose you were going to have brain surgery. When a doctor operates on a brain, it's pretty tricky and he has to be very careful not to do any damage. It is nerve-wracking and there are a lot of problems, but there's one problem the doctor doesn't have. He doesn't have to think that if his knife slips he'll cut your *will* by accident. There is no little part of your brain called "the will".

23

Robin: Well of course not. The will doesn't sit inside your skull the way the heart sits inside your chest. I know that. But still, you do have a free will.

Chris: If you don't have anything inside you which is a will, how can you have something which is a free will? Isn't a free will a will which is free, just the way a brown chair is a chair which is brown? I'd say that you couldn't have a free will if you didn't have a will.

Robin: You just *can't* believe we don't have free will! I mean, you have to believe in free will. You are making choices all the time, and some pretty important ones too. You can't live thinking all those choices just happen.

Chris: You mean I'm *compelled* to believe in free will?

Robin: I mean you should believe in it because it is the only thing that makes sense. I know the will isn't a separate part of the body, like the liver or the heart. It is your whole brain, the way the whole thing works, and free will is the ability to make choices: *free choices*. We think of the different things we can do, and we decide which one we want to, and we act on it.

Jan: It's doing what we want that makes us free?

Robin: Doing what we want makes us feel free. But what free choice means isn't quite that. Our choice is free because we could go either way, and we go the way we want to. The way we decide to. We do decide, ourselves, and we wouldn't need to do this if there were only one possibility. There are alternatives, choices. The reason you have to believe

24

in free will is that it's absolutely obvious that we make free choices. You know free will from the way your own mind works. You are making free choices all the time.

Chris: So you're saying the ability to make free choices is something in the whole person? Or the whole brain, maybe?

Robin: I guess so. It comes when the brain is quite complicated, I suppose. At least complicated enough to see into the future and think of several different actions. I think dogs and cats might have free will — maybe ducks too, fish probably not. I'm not sure and I don't care all that much — not right now, anyway. What I'm interested in is human free will, especially *my* free will. I am sure I have free will. At least a hundred times a day I make choices. What better evidence could I have?

Chris: You make many choices, therefore you have free will. Is that the argument?

Robin: I make many *free* choices; therefore I have free will.

Jan: Saying you have free will doesn't mean you have a thing in you called a will and it is free, then. It just means you can make free choices. Is that it?

Robin: Right. You are making decisions and choices all the time, and they are free choices. So you have free will.

Jan: So what makes a choice free?

Robin: It's free if it could go one way or the other. Say I go off to the mall to the snack bar and I have a dollar. I can buy either ice cream or french fries. It's a choice. I look at the posters and smell the smells and start thinking to myself. So I know I can do the one thing or the other — get french fries, or get ice cream.

Chris: Or neither, for that matter. You could give the money to some worthwhile cause and save on calories.

Jan: So you are making this momentous choice, between ice cream and french fries...

Robin: Suppose I think, 'well it's a cool day and french fries would be pretty good. They are nice and warm. And ice cream might make me feel chilly...'; then I pick french fries. I have made a free choice. I have spent my dollar, of my own free will. I could have bought ice cream or saved the money, or given it to a worthy cause, or whatever. But I didn't. I freely chose to spend it on french fries.

Jan: So you did what you wanted?

Robin: Yes. I did it of my own free will, because I chose to. Nothing made me do it. I wanted to.

Chris: Where did your want come from? I mean, why did you want something warm on a cool day?

Jan: Come on, Chris. You sound like a four-year old. You know, those little kids who are always saying, "Why." 'Why is the sky blue?', 'Why don't trains go on the road?', 'Why do things get old?', stuff like that. My little brother used to do that and it drove me nuts. Don't you start!

Chris: You shouldn't make fun of kids' questions, Jan.

Do you know, someone once told me that the question 'why is the sky dark at night?' is actually very profound. Even the most expert astronomers aren't sure what the answer to it is.

Robin: Maybe, Chris, but the question you asked me isn't like that. I mean, 'why do you want something warm on a cold day?' — for heaven's sake! Isn't it obvious? To keep me warm. I like feeling warm.

Jan: The point is, Robin, what might cause you to make choices. Suppose you make choices based on what you want. You pick something because you want to, so you feel free. Great. But actually your choice is determined — you know, by your wanting one thing instead of another. If your want causes your choice, then your choice has to come out one way rather than the other, because it's caused to be the way it is. And why do you have these wants anyway? They have to come from somewhere.

Chris: That's the point. Everything has a cause. That's a basic assumption of all of science. If scientists didn't study the world, trying to find causes, they wouldn't be able to explain and predict how things work. And you can't ignore science. That's what tells us what our world is like — physics, biology, chemistry, geology, and so on.

Jan: If you went to a doctor with a problem and he just said, "Well, how interesting, here is something for which there is no cause at all," wouldn't you feel mad? You would change doctors pretty fast! Scientists can't assume things just happen for no reason, just randomly. And the rest of us can't either.

Chris: Are you saying science believes in causes, and causes mean there's no free will? That makes sense to me.

Robin: Actually, doctors don't always know causes. If you went with cancer, the doctor might just say it was a random event that you got it. Even with back problems they don't do much better. They don't know causes or cures.

Chris: These things aren't known yet. But some day they will be.

Jan: Cancer probably has all sorts of different causes. But getting back to those french fries...

Robin: Are you hungry?

Jan: A little. But I don't know why. I had a big lunch. Let's just keep talking. Aren't your choices caused, Robin?

Robin: I don't know. I honestly never looked at it that way. If I am doing what I want, like getting french fries, I feel free, and if I have chosen to get them, I think I've made a free choice. But anyway, even if they are caused, why would that show I have no free will? If the causes are right inside me and I am doing what I want, I'm still free.

Chris: You're free in some sense. You aren't coerced by anything. The cause is within yourself, having to do with your own hunger and liking for french fries and wanting to feel warm on a cool day. Nothing outside you makes you buy them, so you think you are free. It's not as though someone is standing beside you with a club, saying "get french fries or I'll bash you one!" Still, though, if wanting to feel warm caused you to pick them, then you couldn't really have done anything else.

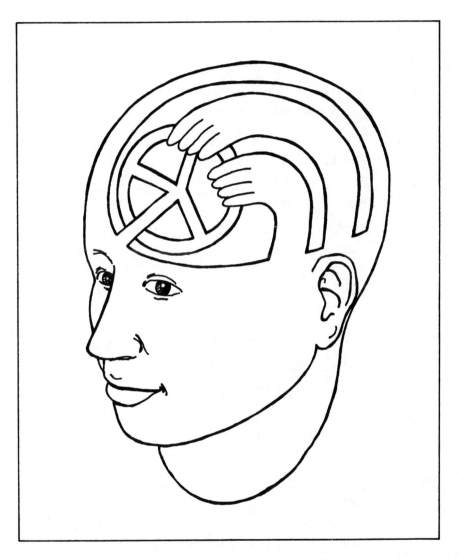

Robin: That's ridiculous. I could have picked whatever I wanted, and I did pick what I wanted, and I was free. Gee, nothing made me want french fries. And I could have picked ice cream, I'm sure I could have. I made a choice between them.

Jan: What about ads for french fries?

Robin: Come on, Jan. What about ads for ice cream? Or ads for staying thin? Or for giving money to Oxfam?

Chris: The point is, is your choice free or isn't it? Even when you feel free, you still don't know what's affecting your choice.

Robin: It's a free choice, because I am doing what I want, according to what I think myself. I am acting from my own mind. So I'm free.

Jan: Haven't you ever heard of psychological compulsions, like kleptomania and so on? People have a mental sickness, something wrong in their minds or brains that gives them an overwhelming desire to steal. If a kleptomaniac goes into a store and walks out with a lot of stuff he hasn't paid for, it's not because he has freely chosen to commit the crime of theft. It's because he *has* to do it. Something in his own make-up just makes him do it.

Chris: This whole thing isn't irrelevant to the french fries choice either. There are such things as compulsive eaters, you know.

Robin: Well I'm not a compulsive eater. I can turn down french fries and other foods whenever I want. It was a free choice. Just because some people have compulsions, that doesn't mean everybody does.

Jan: If a kleptomaniac steals something, acting under a compulsion, what he does is caused by things inside himself. Wants and desires he has, and so on.

But still, it isn't free. So just because you are doing what you want yourself when you buy the french fries, that doesn't prove you are choosing freely.

Chris: Hypnotic suggestion is like this too.

Robin: Hypnotic suggestion is like kleptomania? Weird!

Chris: The thing is, people can be told to do a thing under hypnosis and then after they are normally awake, they do it. They think they have freely and independently chosen it, but they only do it because the hypnotist told them to. My aunt, for instance. Once she let herself be hypnotised by one of those travelling hypnotists who puts on a public show.

Robin: Your Aunt Muriel? I can't believe it! I'd never do that.

Chris: Me either. But Aunt Muriel can surprise you. Anyway, this hypnotist asked for volunteers, and she went on stage along with about twenty other people. They were all standing there looking stunned and literally out of it, and he told them that at 2 o'clock they would stand up, put their coats on, walk to the end of their aisle of seats, face the stage and bow, and then return to their seats. This was at about 1:30. At 1:35, this hypnotist brought the people out of the trance and they all returned to their seats.

Jan: Just a minute, Chris. Did you see this show yourself, or is this just a family story?

Chris: Oh, I was there. She had taken me and my two cousins, but she was the only one of us who had the nerve to go up on the stage. So these volunteers returned to their seats, and we were all just sitting there, listening to this hypnotist lecture about the benefits of hypnosis. When 2 o'clock came, sure enough, all those people who had been on stage did just what he had told them to. It was quite a sight. They all stood up, put on their coats, walked to the aisle, and bowed to the stage. Then they looked around, a little puzzled and embarrassed, and came back to their seats.

Robin: But why? It doesn't seem to make sense!

Chris: It's hard to understand, but hypnotic suggestion apparently works like that. You relax under hypnosis and you accept suggestions made to you. The ideas are somehow stored in the brain. They remain when the hypnotic trance is over, so that you act on them later. That's why some hypnotists think they can cure problems like smoking, drinking, and over-eating. If they can put a powerful enough suggestion in the person, the bad habits will stop.

Jan: I've heard, though, that it's not too successful with deep habits like smoking. And they say a hypnotist can't get a person to do something he wouldn't do ordinarily. I mean, if that hypnotist had told your Aunt Muriel to strip off all her clothes, right on stage, or to put arsenic in the family supper, she wouldn't have done it.

Chris: Let's hope not. The mind isn't like a blank blackboard that the hypnotist can just write any order at all on. The suggestion has to be something that fits in with the person's character, or it won't work.

Robin: I can't imagine your Aunt Muriel in such a

ridiculous situation! What did she say when she found out she had been controlled like a puppet by that hypnotist?

Chris: She did feel a bit silly. You know it can be upsetting to find yourself manipulated like that.

Jan: That's why I'd never let myself be hypnotised. I want to be in charge of my own actions and ideas.

Robin: If you're thinking that way, you should believe in free will.

Chris: The interesting thing about Aunt Muriel, though, was that the choice she made felt to her just like a free choice. It was an everyday, routine thing. It felt free because she didn't know something caused it. She was listening to the lecture and she suddenly had the idea that her parking meter might be running out. She didn't want a ticket, so she put on her coat and started to leave the show to put in some more money. When she got to the aisle, the thought struck her that the show had been great and that if she left early, the hypnotist might be a bit insulted and think she wasn't impressed. On a whim, she bowed to show her respect for his performance. Then she remembered it was a Sunday and there weren't any meter charges on Sunday, so she went back to her seat.

Robin: Along with twenty or so other people who also started to walk out and bow to the hypnotist. Good grief! What kinds of stories did the other people make up to explain their doing such a peculiar thing?

Jan: I wonder. Isn't it amazing how nicely she could

rationalize to cover up such an embarrassing thing?

Chris: The really fascinating thing is that I'm sure she wasn't lying. I mean, she really did think about her parking meter and so on. It's just that her thought and wishes weren't the real cause for her doing what she did. The real cause was the hypnotic suggestion, which was kind of hidden underneath.

Robin: Well it's a great story. I would love to have seen your Aunt Muriel when she figured out what had happened. But still, I don't see what all this is supposed to prove about free will. So, sometimes people think they are making a free choice and they happen to be wrong. Maybe even because a hypnotist put a suggestion into their minds. But so what? We aren't always under the influence of hypnotists. Just because Aunt Muriel didn't freely choose to bow to the stage in this one case doesn't mean that she lacks free will the rest of the time. She made a free choice to go up on the stage with the hypnotist in the first place, didn't she? Most of our choices are free, even if there are bizarre things like kleptomania and eating compulsions and hypnotic suggestions.

Chris: How do you mean they're free? They could go either way? Or there are no outside causes?

Robin: Both.

Jan: I don't think it's quite that simple, Robin. What worries me about this thing with Aunt Muriel is that she could feel so free, and think she knew why she was doing things, and be so wrong! She probably felt just as free getting up and bowing as you did, Robin, when you chose french fries instead of ice cream.

Chris: Right. She felt completely free, but she was only doing it because of what the hypnotist told her.

Jan: It's the rationalizing that worries me. It was so easy for your aunt to come up with these really convincing sounding reasons for why she had to walk out and bow and come back. Maybe we rationalize all the time without knowing it.

Chris: That's the point. At least with this thing about the hypnotist, Aunt Muriel could find out she was wrong, because there were so many of us who had seen what happened. But often it's not so easy. Who knows what's making us do the things we do and choose the things we choose?

Jan: Do you think our ideas and desires are kind of implanted in us, by outside powers?

Robin: Outside powers? You mean, like God or the Devil? Get serious! I can choose french fries without them being involved.

Chris: Seriously, hypnotic suggestion is just the tip of the iceberg. But I wasn't thinking of God making a kind of fate for everyone, like predestination, or of satanic influences or anything like that. I was thinking of the unconscious, you know. Of all the memories and ambitions, and fears, and desires we have but aren't really aware of.

Robin: What do you mean?

Chris: They say 90% of an iceberg is submerged. Freud and other psychiatrists say the same thing about our minds. We have many desires and memories and ideas which we don't even know exist. They work underneath our surface conscious ideas and they affect what we do, even when we aren't aware of it. You don't need a hypnotist to be deceived about your reasons for acting. Your own unconscious mind can be working on you!

Robin: So that's what Freud thought? Well, good for him. But that doesn't prove it's true. These psychiatrists disagree with each other all the time. Remember John Hinckley, who attempted to assassinate President Reagan? There were four psychiatrists at his trial. One said he suffered from schizophrenia, another said he didn't suffer from schizophrenia, a third said he had a very severe depressive disorder, and a fourth said there was little evidence that he was depressed. So what do these people know? They all disagree. I don't see why I should stop believing in my own free will just because of what psychiatrists say. I still think that a person usually knows best what his own reasons for doing things are. If I think about my reasons for deciding to have french fries, and I deliberately choose to spend a dollar and get some, I feel as though I am choosing freely and doing what I want. And usually, I *am*. That's why I have free will.

Jan: Maybe, but that's such a boring example, if you don't mind my saying so. Think of something more serious. You know, like mothers who rush around doing things for their children and think they are doing them out of love and concern, whereas really they have a subconscious guilt or desire to make themselves into victims. Don't people sometimes misunderstand their own motives? You can't just say psychiatrists don't know anything. A lot of people go to them for years and get lots of help with their problems.

Robin: If they get so much help, why do they have to keep going for years?

Chris: I think we're getting off the track with Freud and all this stuff. The problem really is with the causes for us doing what we do. First Robin thought that if the causes were events in a person's own brain, that would mean the choice was free. Nothing outside would be making her act, so she would be free. But that can't be right, because with kleptomaniacs and other people acting from compulsive disorders, and with people acting under hypnotic suggestion, like Aunt Muriel, the causes are in their own brains, and yet the choices are not free. There are times when people are compelled to choose the way they do, even if what compels them is something inside themselves. Even though they feel quite free, the choice isn't really free.

Robin: Provided it's true that it must go one way rather than the other. The real question is whether there are alternatives. It sure feels like there are, and I still think there are.

Jan: Wait a minute. We keep talking as if there is just one cause for our choice and our problem is to find out what that one cause is. But nothing has just one cause. Everything that happens has many causes, going far far back in time. If one event is caused by an earlier event, that earlier event is caused by a still earlier one, and so on and so on and so on. So a person's decision is really preceded by a whole chain of related events that goes way far back in time.

Robin: *How* far back? When does it stop?

Chris: Logically, you would have to say never. It goes back as far as time itself. If time is infinite, there is an infinite series of causes before every event.

Robin: There's an infinite series of causes preceding my decision to get french fries? An infinite series can never be finished, so if there had to be one, I couldn't have picked the french fries at all!

Jan: It doesn't work that way. Look, I don't know whether time goes back forever and I don't think anybody else does either. If every event has a cause, then the cause of an event, which is another event, obviously has a cause, and its cause will have a cause too, and so on. The order of causes must go back at least as far as the universe itself.

Chris: Let's say Robin chooses fries because of wanting something warm on a cool day and this wanting is some kind of thing happening in her brain. Then there would be causes for what happens in her brain, and causes for those causes, and so on. It would go right back to the beginning of the universe.

Jan: Right. So even if a choice comes from within yourself, within the brain, it comes from outside causes too. And those outside causes can't be controlled by a person. Your choices don't just spring from your own self alone. It's just not true.

Chris: It seems as if everything must fall into a chain of

causes. At the beginning of the universe there was a Creation, or some *Big Bang* kind of event, and from then on causes just go on and on unfolding, without anybody being able to do anything about it. Even if you think God caused the whole thing, once the universe got started, it just kept on going.

Robin: This is getting too spooky for words. I mean, really, thinking that choosing french fries would be an effect of causes that go back millions or billions of years to some *Big Bang* that might have been the beginning of the universe! It's absurd! Anyway, I've heard that scientists don't even believe in complete causes any more. For electrons and the smallest particles of matter, there are random unpredictable happenings.

Chris: Well I don't know. But having random electrons in your brain wouldn't give you free will anyway, would it? I mean, if they are moving here and there and nobody can predict where they will be, it doesn't make your decision more free. Because you wouldn't be in control of what's happening.

Robin: I guess not. But if science is saying uncaused events can happen, at least on the level of electrons and smaller particles, then science isn't as committed to causation as you've been saying. The world isn't all tied up in causal chains.

Chris: Most science is still causal.

Robin: Look, maybe it makes sense to think of all these ordered causes for physical events like the rain falling and the wind blowing and avalanches and so on. But you're over-simplifying science. When you get down to the micro level, things aren't all ordered and caused. And complete causes for people's actions? I don't think so. Here you are, telling me that a simple decision by a person has an infinite series of causes.

Chris: It has to be that way, Robin. Things don't just pop out of nothing and nowhere.

Robin: Chris, you think you're so sensible, but this is wild, really wild. You're telling me every simple decision has got to have an infinite set of causes. And yet you don't even know what causes one simple choice. And neither does anyone else. Psychologists and psychiatrists don't agree on the causes of even one single simple human decision. They really don't. If they knew the causes of choices and actions, we could predict what people will do. And we just can't. Not even for the most trivial things.

Chris: I said it before and I'll say it again. Every event has a cause so whatever Robin does has to have a cause. Even if we don't know yet what that cause is. Then, given it's caused, it can only go one way. The cause determines it to be this way and not the other. If Robin chose french fries, there was a cause for her choosing them, and given that cause, she had to choose them. Robin said free will means your choice can go either way. But if that's what it means, there is just no such thing as free will.

Jan: Now you've gone too far. I'm starting to agree with Robin. You keep insisting every event has a cause, like it's some kind of basic truth or something. But scientists *don't* know every event has a cause. And nobody else does either. Sure, maybe scientists assume causation, generally, but even that's only for some parts of science, not all. And the assumption could turn out to be wrong.

Chris: There are things we can't predict, sure. Like cancer, or back problems, or even the weather. But these things must have causes and in principle they can be predicted. Some day, someone will know the cause and will be able to make predictions, even for human decisions about french fries and ice cream.

Jan: And more profound ones too, I hope — like whether to get married, or enlist in an army, or become a doctor?

Chris: Of course.

Robin: Chris, you have real faith, you really do. I always thought of you as a kind of down-to-earth sensible person. But you have this amazing faith and confidence in science. And you have such confidence that the universe is a rational place where everything will make sense. Look around you. Does the world make sense?

Jan: Make sense to whom?

Chris: Think about it, Robin. Suppose that some human decision is not caused. Then it would be just random. It would come about for no reason at all. It would sort of emerge — *poof!* — from what existed before. This would be weird, for sure. And it still wouldn't give you real freedom when you act. Say there is a neuron in your brain and an electron in the neuron which makes a random motion. That doesn't make you a free agent! How would it give

41

you free will?

Robin: I would freely decide. My decision wouldn't be completely caused, and it couldn't be predicted from the state of my brain at the moment just before I made it.

Chris: That's just randomness. It isn't freedom.

Jan: That's not fair, Chris. Robin didn't say that human actions happen randomly. The point was, we don't know yet what causes them. And maybe we never will know. If we don't know the cause of even one single simple human action, then why should we insist that every human action has causes going right back to the beginning of the universe?

Chris: Robin, you're right to say we don't know these causes. Human beings seem much harder to figure out than rocks and rain and wind. But just because we don't know the causes, that doesn't mean those causes don't exist, and it doesn't mean that they won't be known some day by somebody.

Jan: We agreed on that when we were talking about sperm and worms, didn't we? If one sperm unites with an egg and another one doesn't, we don't know the full explanation. We don't know why it was that particular sperm which resulted in us, and not some other sperm, resulting in a whole different person. But our ignorance doesn't prove the sperm made a free choice. If one worm comes up on the lawn in the morning and another doesn't, well, OK, we don't know why. But our ignorance about the explanation doesn't prove there is no cause, and it certainly doesn't prove that worms have free will. The same argument holds for human beings. Sure, the causes aren't known, but that doesn't prove you have free will.

Robin: Sure, it doesn't *prove* it. But the possibility is still there. The point is, human beings are not sperm and we are not worms either. We know what we are doing, and we know why we choose things. We have complicated brains and we are aware of having alternatives and making choices. We think about what we are going to do, and we examine reasons, and we pick. We do know we are doing this. And we *know* we sometimes decide to do one thing when we could have done others. That's what it means to have free will. It is just plain common sense. People have free will.

Jan: But it used to be common sense that the world was flat. Everybody knew it. There was just one problem: they turned out to be wrong. I don't know how much you can rely on your so-called common sense to tell you that free will is real.

Chris: Remember Aunt Muriel. She relied on her common sense too. She just knew she was leaving the theater to go out and put some money in her parking meter. Then it turned out she was wrong.

Robin: That's different. Aunt Muriel let herself be hypnotised. She did what she did because of hypnotic suggestion. But we aren't all like Aunt Muriel all the time, and we aren't all like kleptomaniacs or psychiatric patients all the time either. We feel and we think and we choose, and we know what we're doing. We have choices to make, and we make them. That is acting freely, of our own free will, and every single person on this earth has tons of evidence every day that he or she can do this.

To me, this shows we should believe in free will.

Jan: Could scientists ever prove you're wrong, the way they did with the flat earth theory? After all, people had tons of evidence that the earth was flat. They walked on it, and looked at it, and so on, and it didn't seem like a globe. It seemed like a flat surface. Then Columbus set off west from Spain in 1492 and proved it wasn't.

Chris: Was it Spain? I thought it was Portugal.

Jan: Well, it doesn't really matter. The point is that common sense wisdom about the earth being flat turned out to be just plain wrong. And the same could happen to Robin's common sense ideas about free will.

Robin: Look Jan, maybe psychologists or other scientists *will* someday prove there is no free will, I don't know. But they haven't proved it yet. Chris keeps saying that every event must have a cause. But we don't know this. It's just an assumption, and not even an assumption for all of science. Most scientists don't believe it's true for small particles of things, like electrons. What I don't see is why this merely probable *assumption*, which doesn't even hold all the time, should make me question my own experience of freedom.

Chris: You're just arguing from ignorance, Robin. What you're saying amounts to no more than the idea that because scientists don't know the causes of human actions, people have free will.

Jan: That's not quite it.

Robin: That's certainly *not* it. I'm saying that because no one has established causes for human actions and decisions, I'm entitled to believe what my experience tells me about my own choices. And my experience tells me that I choose freely between real alternatives. There is just no compelling argument that I should change my mind.

Jan: So for now you're free to believe in free will?

Robin: Right. And I'm quite determined to go on doing it!

GOD, THE DEVIL, AND THE PERFECT PIZZA

Jan: Did you know you can prove the existence of God by pure logic?

Chris: Come on, Jan. Believing in God is a matter of faith and emotion. You don't get true religion from pure logic.

Robin: Sounds neat. How does it go?

Jan: I just heard about it the other day. The proof comes from a scholar who lived in the Middle Ages. His name was Anselm, and he said it was a contradiction to deny that God exists. Since logic forbids contradictions, logic will tell you that God exists.

Chris: Isn't that nice of logic! I'll believe it when I see it.

Jan: It goes like this: you start with an understanding of what God is. God is a unique, perfect being, a being greater than which none can be conceived.

Robin: What a mouthful! It hardly makes sense. Being greater than which none can be conceived? What is that supposed to mean?

Jan: It isn't really that hard. God has to be the Greatest Conceivable Being because you can't imagine a being greater than God. No greater being can be conceived. He or She is the Greatest, the

Most Perfect.

Chris: I'll bet they didn't refer to God as He or She in St. Anselm's day. But anyway, what does "conceived" mean?

Jan: Something like "imagined" or "understood in the mind." To say that God is the Greatest Conceivable Being is to say that when a human tries to grasp or understand a very great being, then the very greatest one that human reason can come up with is God. God is the Greatest in our minds, and the Greatest in the real world too. It has to be that way. That's just what God is.

Robin: Just a minute. How did the real world get into all this? You might have an idea of God, I don't know, but if you do, it's only in your mind.

Chris: Right. And anyway, this is all just words. You haven't given us any argument.

Robin: Patience is a virtue, Chris, whether you believe in God or not. Hang on a minute.

Jan: Here's the argument. God is the Greatest Conceivable Being. Now let us suppose that God, defined this way, does not exist in the real world, but only in our minds. If He or She does not exist in the real world, then there is one important feature lacking, and that is the feature of existence in the real world. Existence in the real world is part of greatness and perfection. If the Greatest Conceivable Being did not exist in reality, but only in our minds, then we would be able to imagine or conceive a Being even greater than Him or Her.

Robin: Existing in the real world is greater than existing

only in the mind?

Jan: Right. So, if the Greatest Being you could conceive only existed in your mind, and didn't exist in reality, then there would be a Greater Being. That would be one just the same, but with one additional feature: existence in reality. Now the second being would be Greater than the first one, because it would have all the same qualities plus one more: existence in reality. Not just in our minds, in reality. That means that if the Greatest Conceivable Being did not exist, there would be another being greater than the Greatest Conceivable Being. This would be the Greatest Conceivable Being, so God would still exist.

Robin: That doesn't make sense. Nothing can be Greater than the Greatest. The Greatest has to be the most Great, because that's just what "greatest" means.

Jan: Right. That's what the argument depends on. You can't have a being which is Greater than the Greatest Conceivable Being. It would be a contradiction.

Chris: Logic doesn't allow contradictions.

Jan: Right. You get a contradiction from supposing that the Greatest Conceivable Being — that is, God — does not exist. You can't accept that contradiction, so you have to reject the idea that led to the contradiction. And what was that? It was the claim that God does not exist. If you reject the idea that God *does not* exist, then you have admitted that God *does* exist. See? You can prove that God exists.

48

Robin: He exists because it's a contradiction to say He doesn't?

Chris: He or She, you mean.

Robin: All right, all right. Jan, have I got it right?

Jan: I think so. If the Greatest Conceivable Being did not exist in reality, there would be a greater being still, one which did exist in reality — not just in the mind. That Being would be Greater than the Greatest, which is a contradiction. We cannot accept a contradiction. Therefore the Greatest Conceivable Being exists in reality as well as in the mind. God exists. No one who understands what God is can really believe that He doesn't exist.

Chris: Was it St. Anselm who once said that "only the fool says in his heart that God does not exist?"

Jan: I think so.

Robin: I guess he meant that only a fool would believe a contradiction.

Jan: Maybe. He thought that if you really understood the idea of God as the Greatest Conceivable Being, then, once you had this idea in your mind, you could understand that God must exist. God is a complete being, not depending on anything else. He couldn't be a perfect being if He didn't exist in reality. So that's how you prove God's existence from pure logic. Neat, isn't it?

Robin: Maybe one problem is that not everyone has this overwhelming idea of a perfect, powerful, independent God in his mind in the first place.

Chris: To me it sounds fishy. You start out with an idea

of God and a definition and the principle that you can't allow contradictions, and you wind up accepting that God exists. It just can't be that easy!

Jan: There is a great story about Bertrand Russell and this argument. That's what they call it, the Ontological Argument. Well anyway, Russell says in his autobiography that one day he was riding along on his bicycle at Cambridge University and he suddenly thought to himself, "Great Scott, the Ontological Argument is valid!"

Chris: That must have been when Russell was quite young. He didn't go on believing in it, did he?

Robin: He can't have, because he later wrote a famous book called *Why I Am Not a Christian*.

Jan: So Russell changed his mind. I wonder why.

Chris: Russell was sensible enough to see that there has to be something wrong with that argument. I don't know, I mean he did all this technical logic, and I think it had something to do with that. Oh yeah, I think he said the ontological argument makes God a necessary being, and only statements can be necessary. I don't know, something like that, but I'm not sure what he meant.

Robin: It sounds obscure.

Chris: That's for sure. The way I see it, the real problem is that Anselm seems to assume that we can understand what the Greatest Conceivable Being is. I don't think we can at all. I can't imagine what the Greatest Conceivable Being would be like.

Robin: Anselm argues that if God exists in your mind,

then He or She has to exist in reality too. But what if God doesn't even exist in your mind? What happens to the argument then? How can we imagine God?

Jan: Well I don't think you're supposed to be able to imagine Him or Her, in the sense of having an image or anything. I mean you're not supposed to be able to see God in all glory right in your mind's eye.

Chris: I know that, but isn't it going a bit far to assume that people have a grasp of what God is, or that they can understand the Greatest Conceivable Being?

Jan: If people don't have an idea of God, what do they think of when they use the word "God," then? Some people believe in God and others don't. To even wonder whether God exists, you have to have some idea of God. God has to exist at least in your mind, and that's where St. Anselm's argument begins. You can't just say that people don't have any idea of God. There are lots and lots of people who certainly *seem* to have one. Why can't St. Anselm assume that people have an idea of God when he's making the Ontological Argument? Every argument has to start somewhere!

Robin: But starting from the idea of God is a bit more than just starting somewhere, isn't it? It's a pretty special idea, you have to admit. How are we supposed to be able to get this idea? Is it born in us or something?

Jan: Maybe we get the idea of a completely perfect being when we see how inadequate we are oursel-

51

ves. You know, we get it as a sort of opposite of our own guilt and our own imperfection. That makes us think of perfect power and greatness.

Chris: I don't see how anyone could have a real understanding of what the Greatest Conceivable Being is.

Robin: I bet that even St. Anselm probably would have found the thought that a mere human being could completely understand the idea of God quite insulting to God. It would be blasphemy to say that a mere human could fully understand what God is.

Chris: Well, right, that was my point.

Jan: But still, I think Anselm's Ontological Argument can work. We do understand the idea of the Greatest Conceivable Being to some extent. All we need for the argument, really, is the idea that there can't be a Being Greater than the Greatest. It is just a matter of simple logic with Greater and Greatest. That's enough to make the argument work.

Robin: Still, something is wrong with it. Something just *has* to be wrong with it. Suppose I give you this argument, which seems just the same. Imagine the greatest conceivable pizza. Now suppose this pizza does not exist in reality, but only in the mind. If it doesn't exist in reality, there must be another pizza with all the same qualities, except that it exists both in reality and in the mind. This second pizza would be greater than the greatest, which is a contradiction. You get a contradiction if you assume that the Greatest Conceivable Pizza does not exist in reality. Therefore it must exist. Somewhere in this world there is a Greatest Conceivable Pizza.

Chris: Wonderful! I wonder whether it's pepperoni or Hawaian or what.

Robin: That must depend on who's conceiving it. Hey, maybe there are as many different Greatest Conceivable Pizzas as there are people imagining them! Then nobody would have to be hungry any more — provided they like pizza!

Chris: Maybe there are as many different gods as there are people imagining them too.

Jan: Come on, Chris, you can't compare God to a pizza. That is really insulting.

Chris: Look, it's the very same argument for the pizza and for God. Obviously we aren't going to believe in a Super-Pizza on the basis of this argument, so we shouldn't believe in God on the basis of the Ontological Argument either.

Robin: If we did accept these kinds of arguments we could prove the existence of a whole super-world. The Greatest Conceivable Man with the Greatest Conceivable Woman and their Greatest Conceivable House, Baby, Music, Art, Philosophy, and so on.

Jan: That's not fair, Robin. God is unique. The idea of God is special.

Chris: I think Robin's right. This is madness. Does the greatest conceivable philosophy include the Ontological Argument as part of it? For heaven's sake, surely an argument must be wrong if you could use it to prove the existence of a whole super-world.

Jan: So if your pizza argument is the same as the Ontological Argument, there must be something wrong with the Ontological Argument. But I'm not sure it is the same. Surely the case of God is special, because the idea of God is the idea of a completely perfect, completely powerful, absolutely great being. It's not like your idea of a perfect pizza. For heaven's sake!

Robin: No pun intended of course, Jan. Eh?

Chris: Jan, it's the same argument, the very same. You start with the idea of the greatest conceivable something or other, whether it's the greatest conceivable being or the greatest conceivable pizza or the greatest conceivable philosophy. Then you suppose it doesn't exist, deduce a contradiction, and then, by rejecting the contradiction, prove the thing exists. Doing this, you can prove a whole super-world.

Jan: Something *is* wrong with the Ontological Argument, then. But what? Where is the mistake?

Robin: Let's not move too fast here. Maybe you can save the Ontological Argument by saying that there is something unique and special about the idea of God as the Greatest Conceivable Being. I mean, this idea is more special and important than ideas of pizzas and men and women and so on. Isn't that what Anselm would say if he were here?

Chris: Spirit of Anselm, wherever you are, aren't you glad not to be here!

Jan: I think somebody once criticized St. Anselm by drawing a comparison with a perfect island. Anselm tried to defend his argument by saying the idea of God was special.

Chris: Sure, sure. Of course he wanted to hang on to his argument. But how can you be consistent and accept the argument about the Greatest Conceivable Being if you are going to reject the Greatest Conceivable Island and the Greatest Conceivable Pizza and so on? It's just arbitrary. People should base their religion on faith instead of playing around with these so-called proofs. Religion depends on your feelings and your experiences, not on all this playing around with words.

Jan: I think Anselm said that we do have this idea of a Greatest Conceivable Being, whereas we don't have the other ideas. We have this idea of God as completely perfect, and as not depending on anything else outside Him for His existence. He *has* to exist. He has necessary existence.

Chris: Now *that* reminds me of Russell, and it's just what he was objecting to. That whole bit about necessary existence. It just doesn't make sense.

Robin: Isn't there necessary existence in mathematics? You know, you can prove by logic there are an infinite number of prime numbers and all that. Infinity necessarily exists. Maybe God is a necessary being kind of the way numbers are.

Chris: You can't mean that, Robin. Where do we get this idea of this completely perfect Necessary Being from, anyway?

Robin: From God, I guess. He or She makes sure we are all equipped with an idea of Him or Her so that we can figure out that God exists.

Chris: But then we have to assume God exists in order to make St. Anselm's argument work, and his argument is supposed to prove that God exists. A good argument can't assume exactly what it's supposed to prove!

Jan: That's not the point, Chris. The thing is, for a religious person, the idea of God is the idea of a completely overwhelming Being. Once you get the idea, it's impossible to think God does not exist.

Robin: I just had another idea. Maybe you can use the

56

Ontological Argument to prove the existence of the Devil.

Jan: Boy, Robin, your imagination is really working overtime today. First perfect pizzas, now the Devil!

Chris: I don't think St. Anselm meant it to work that way. Gosh, if he had been keen on proving the existence of the Devil, I don't think they would have made him a saint.

Robin: Maybe not, but think about it. Let us define the Devil as the Worst Conceivable Being. Now suppose he does not exist in reality, but only in the mind. Then there could be an even worse being, one just like the first but which exists in reality as well as in the mind. So if the Devil doesn't exist, you could have a being worse than the Devil, which would be a being worse than the worst conceivable being. And that is a contradiction; therefore the Devil must exist in reality as well as in the mind. It is just like the other argument except that you wind up proving the Devil instead of God.

Chris: Good grief! But is it just the same — I mean, logically? In the Ontological Argument, St. Anselm said that lacking existence in reality would be a deficiency for God. I mean that for God existing in reality is better than existing in the mind only. But in this argument about the Devil, you need to assume that having existence in reality would be an aspect of his 'worseness' for the Devil. The Devil would be worse existing in reality than existing only in the mind.

Robin: Well isn't that true? The Devil *would* be worse

existing in reality than if he only existed in people's minds. He couldn't do nearly as much harm if he only existed in people's minds as he could if he really existed.

Jan: Maybe just the very idea of the Devil does plenty of harm.

Robin: The real thing would be worse yet.

Chris: That's not the point. Look, I don't believe in the Ontological Argument for God or in your argument for the Devil. Maybe they are the same, but they're both worthless.

Robin: Well, don't be dogmatic or anything.

Chris: They are neat arguments, like those paradoxes. You know, the ones about people who always lie and whether they tell you the truth if they say they are lying, that kind of thing. The thing is, there is a difference, because in the Ontological Argument for God, having existence was assumed to be something a Greatest Being would have. For Him or Her, existence would be a good quality. Whereas for the Devil, existence would be terrible, so it's said to be a bad quality. The worst conceivable Being would have to exist in reality, because if he didn't, another one would be even worse. Namely one which had all the features of the first and existence in reality too. It's a contradiction to be worse than the worst, just as it's a contradiction to be Greater than the Greatest. Something has definitely gone wrong.

Jan: I'm not sure there is a problem, Chris. Maybe you and Robin are right. There really is a parallel, and the difference about existence, whether it is a good quality or not, doesn't have to make the parallel inaccurate. Obviously, Anselm assumed that for God existence would be a good thing. But whether existence is a good quality depends on what it is that is supposed to have or lack existence. I mean, since God is good, for God to exist is good, and existence is one of God's good qualities. And since the Devil is evil, for the Devil to exist is bad, and existence is one of the Devil's bad qualities. It seems to work out fine.

Robin: Jan, I can't believe you're saying this. Do you really think we can prove the existence both of God and of the Devil, by pure logic?

Jan: I don't know. The thing about the Devil isn't completely crazy, when you think about it. I mean, maybe if we could bring St. Anselm down from heaven and ask him, he would even approve of this addition to his theory. After all, religious people quite often *do* believe there is a real devil, and probably most people in Anselm's society thought this. Even today, lots of people see world events in terms of a competition between good and evil. That book *The Late Great Planet Earth* sold millions of copies. You know, the one about how evil is battling good and all the good people are going to get 'raptured' up to heaven when the end of the world comes? They believe in supernatural forces of good and evil. You could use the Ontological Argument for God and for the Devil, and you would have a proof for the good force and one for the evil one.

Chris: The world as a competition between good and

evil? For heaven's sake, Jan, it sounds like one of those corny adventure stories. I honestly don't think that serious minded Christians today believe there is a real live Devil out there, leading the forces of evil in the world!

Jan: What about star wars and the evil empire?

Robin: What about "selling yourself to the Devil"? Preachers are always telling us not to do it. They must think there is a devil.

Chris: It's just a figure of speech. I mean, it is just a way of criticizing people for having the wrong values and so on. People who say this don't actually mean there is a real devil.

Jan: I think it depends on who you're talking to. Some people do believe in a real devil, but others just talk that way. Still, I don't think it refutes the Ontological Argument to find out we can make up a similar argument for the existence of the devil. So, we might have two proofs instead of one. The conclusion that the devil exists is one that many Christians would accept, even though they might not use an Ontological Argument for it.

Robin: Jan, I'm amazed. I usually think of you as such a rational careful thinker. And how here you are, telling me you can prove by pure logic the existence of God and the Devil. Not to mention the Perfect Pizza, the Perfect Man, Woman, House, Child and heaven knows what else.

Chris: Hey! Maybe we have a brand new definition of Heaven from all this. Heaven would be where all these greatest conceivable things are.

Robin: And hell where all the worst conceivable ones are? There must be a worst conceivable pizza too, by the same argument. Right?

Jan: You two aren't being fair. I never said I thought the arguments were right. All I said was I thought they were neat and interesting. And I think they are parallel to each other. Logically, I mean.

Robin: And you think it is all right to be able to prove the existence of the Devil as well as God.

Jan: Well, I don't think that completely refutes Anselm's argument.

Chris: There just has to be something wrong. I mean, we still have that little matter of the perfect pizza. Surely you aren't going to say that we can prove by pure logic that the Greatest Conceivable Pizza exists! Or worse yet that millions of Greatest Conceivable Pizzas exist, one for everybody who conceives one.

Jan: No, that's crazy. You can't just take an idea, get a definition, and then fool around with some logical rules and then wind up knowing things exist. I mean, the Perfect Pizza might exist in your mind, but that doesn't mean it exists outside your mind!

Robin: It doesn't even exist in your stomach. Too bad!

Chris: Jan, now you're getting to it, but I think you just gave away the whole show. I mean, that *is* the problem. We can't just define things into existence. The Ontological Argument just has to be the height of human arrogance. Reason is something in the human mind and it can't show us what is outside the mind.

Robin: You mean it's there sometimes. Reason isn't in every human mind.

Chris: Don't distract me. You know what I mean. Reason is in us, and it is not in the world outside us. Our definitions are just things we make up. We can't get knowledge about what is outside just by definitions and reasoning. We have to experience things. We have to be in contact with a real world, one which is outside ourselves. You are only going to find out there's a perfect pizza if you experience it—you know, if you really find one, out there in the real world of cheese and batter and spices and restaurants. You don't find out there's a perfect pizza just by doing logic and working out an argument. Obviously you don't find out God exists that way either.

Jan: You mean you're only going to find out there's a perfect pizza if you get to eat it?

Robin: By the time you've finished, you won't know it's the Greatest Conceivable Pizza, because the pizza will be gone. The most you could know is that there *was* a perfect pizza.

Chris: Come on, Robin, be serious.

Robin: I am serious. Experiencing something doesn't tell you all about it. You have to have words and ideas, and you need logic to reason and think about what your experience means. With this pizza thing, you need your reason to see that merely eating a great pizza won't tell you you have found the Greatest Conceivable Pizza. Reason tells you you'd need to eat the whole thing to know how perfect it was. By the time you finished doing that, the pizza would be gone. Anyway, by the time you finished the last bite, you wouldn't remember exactly what the first bites were like, and you wouldn't even know for sure that it had been a perfect pizza. Or the greatest conceivable pizza.

Chris: After you finished, the proof for the perfect pizza would still be valid. So as soon as you ate one, logic would guarantee the existence of another one. Just like that. Poof!

Jan: You can't mean that.

Chris: Of course not. It just shows the argument wasn't valid in the first place.

Robin: But what about God and the Devil? I mean, these are the important subjects.

Chris: The thing is, just looking, hearing, touching, smelling, or tasting something doesn't tell us what that thing is like. Not all by itself, anyway. We need words to classify and relate and compare things, and we need logic so that we can reason about things and avoid contradictions. But the Ontological Argument makes us get too much from just words and logic. That's why I think it's so arrogant. The mind can't make the world.

Jan: There must be something wrong with the Ontological Argument. The idea of proving God's existence from logic alone is quite neat. But you can't really do it. If you could, you could do too many other crazy proofs too. It's fun to think about, but it really doesn't make sense.

Robin: So you're giving up?

Jan: Sure. Well, I never really accepted the whole thing, you know. I just thought it was interesting. Still, there is something that bothers me about this whole business. In the Ontological Argument, we take an idea of God, which we seem to have in our minds — at least some of us do — and we use perfectly normal principles of logic to do some reasoning. We get the conclusion that God exists. Then we find we can take another idea, use the same principles of logic, go through a similar kind of reasoning, and get the conclusion that the Devil exists. We think we can't know these conclusions by reason alone, so we say there's something wrong with our arguments.

Chris: That's it, all right. So what's the matter? That's what we all seem to be agreeing on. I can't see that there's anything the matter with it.

Jan: The problem is that whenever we reason about anything, we have to use our ideas and words and definitions and the normal rules of logic. Usually, you know, in mathematics proofs and so on, we trust these. We get a conclusion and we say, "yeah, this is it." We don't turn around and decide that even though we have what seems to be a perfect proof, we must be wrong anyway.

Robin: The Ontological Argument does sound convincing when you first hear it, doesn't it? And it was good enough for Bertrand Russell.

Chris: Not for long, it wasn't. I don't think the argument sounds convincing, not even at first. To me it sounds like somebody just fooling around with words.

Robin: If we agree that these arguments *are* no good, it doesn't make much sense to dispute about whether they *seem* good, does it? I mean, for Pete's sake, how much arguing do we have to do?

Jan: Not much more. I'll give up soon. What bothers me is that we usually assume we can use words to describe things and ideas and we can put these words into sentence and use basic logic, and reason, and get sensible conclusions. Now it seems that we do all that and we don't get sensible conclusions, at least not for the perfect pizza and all that. My confidence in language and logic is a bit shaken, that's all.

Chris: That's *all*? It sounds serious.

Jan: The whole thing still puzzles me, really.

Robin: I'm exhausted. Come on, let's go get a pizza and think about something else for a while.

Chris: Can we get the Greatest Conceivable Pizza?

Robin: No, the greatest cheap pizza. I've only got six dollars.

MY BRILLIANT
MATHEMATICAL CAREER

I always liked math. When you got the right answer, it was absolutely, perfectly right, and you could prove it. No ifs, buts, howevers...no pros and cons. It came easy to me, and I used to tutor other people too. It was so satisfying to explain the stuff. You could get right to the bottom of things, where it was clear, absolutely crystal clear.

In fact, I nearly went into mathematics, for a career. I loved it, and found it so easy. Everybody said you could make a good living with math because it was part of so many other things. Like physics and engineering — and computing, of course.

It's funny how some people just don't take to mathematics. Like my old friend Rob. Boy, did Rob hate math! Even when we were still in school, he used to bug me about it. He said it was too abstract and it was just arbitrary how the rules went, and it wasn't about anything real. Rob couldn't even get long division, and when it came to x's and y's and similar triangles and negative numbers — well, forget it. I used to try to tutor Rob, but it was just about hopeless. He even used to argue with me about things. As if there is any room for opinions and arguments in mathematics!

I'll never forget the day we got into this stupid argument about Roman numerals. I mean, can you imagine — this is grade five level stuff. We were talking about '5' and 'V' and I was saying there were two different numerals for one number, five. It's simple enough! But not for Rob. He said he could understand well enough what numerals were, that was OK, but as for numbers as such, well they weren't real things at all. Sure, he said, I could write '5' or 'V' or words like "five" or "cinq", but the actual number, five, was not the same as any of these. He wanted to know what was the number itself and where in the world were we supposed to find it?

Well, this was too much. It got to the point I was showing him my hand and his and pointing out we both had the same number of fingers on a hand and that number was five. Kindergarten! Rob said he could see two hands, all right, but five-ness wasn't part of them.

I couldn't get what he meant, really. I mean, the guy was right out of touch. He was smart at other things, things that didn't involve math. As for me, all the numbers made sense to me. You could see two and three make five, you could understand counting, and addition as a function of counting. Then multiplying was just adding, over and over. Subtracting was the reverse of adding. Dividing, the reverse of multiplying. You could experience how all these things worked. You could even experience fractions, with dividing pies in 12 and adding 1/3 of the pie to 1/4 and so on. I never had trouble with negative numbers either. I mean, you could relate them to obvious things like debt. If you have a debt of twenty dollars, and I take it away, then I make you twenty dollars richer, right? So it makes perfect sense for minus a minus to give you plus.

Geometry was terrific. All those proofs, no opinions, it was great. You drew a triangle that wasn't just itself, but represented any triangle at all and had all those nice axioms and relations from that old Greek, Euclid. And then there was algebra. Some people didn't like the x and y, but it was neat, they could represent any number. Those problems about 'John is 1/3 as old as his father was three years ago; his father was 21 when John was born; how old is John?'...I used to love them. I always aced the tests. Rob would get distracted, thinking about whether John's father married too young, and stuff like that. Irrelevant!

There were times when some of the rules in math bothered people who wanted more reasons for them. Not just Rob, even other people who weren't so hopeless about math. There was zero, for instance, and the things you did with it. Zero is a number. It's the number of oranges you have if you start with one and I take it away. Even babies know that! There's none left. So, OK, you have the positive numbers and the negative numbers, and zero is right in between. Obviously. But what bugged people was when you multiplied and divided by zero. You multiply any number by zero, you get zero. It makes sense, doesn't it? Whatever the number, if you take it zero times, you don't have anything. Zero. Zero times anything is zero. Except infinity, maybe.

Dividing by zero is a little harder. Well, sort of. What's harder is, you can't do it. If you try to divide by zero, the answer is "undefined," Mrs. Samuels (that was our teacher) said. Oh yeah, and if you raise anything to the power zero, you get one.

These things were a little funny — peculiar funny, I mean. But you could kind of see it, I thought, especially the business of dividing by zero. Since zero is nothing, then if you ask how many times it goes into a certain number, say 10, then you are asking how many times nothing goes into 10. Well, that doesn't make much sense. You could say, since zero isn't anything, it will go into any quantity an infinite number of times. But that is a bit weird. They leave it "undefined". It made sense to me. But Rob said, "I told you. It's all arbitrary. They just set it up the way they want and make us learn it. Mathematics is a plot of the old against the young." Good grief.

As for things to the power zero — you know, like 2 raised to the zero, 10 raised to the zero, and so on. All of them are equal to one, that's how it's defined. This seems OK, once you get used to it, even though it might seem a little odd at first. See, 2 raised to the third power is 2 times 2 times 2; 2 raised to the fourth power is 2 times 2 times 2 times 2, and so on. For each power, you write the number raised to the power just that number of times to get the answer. This would make you think that 2 raised to the zero power would be zero. You would get the answer by writing 2 zero times, which would seem to give you zero. Wouldn't that be logical?

But they don't say that; it isn't right. Two raised to the zero power is equal to 1 and so is any other number raised to the zero. Why is this? If it weren't this way, you couldn't use some other basic rules. Like the rule of adding exponents when you are multiplying. If you multiply 2 to the 3rd power by 2 to the 2nd power, you get 2 to the 5th power; you add the two powers. If you make 2 to the zero power equal to 1, this rule will still work, because when multiplying 2 to the zero by 2 to the something else, you add the zero, and that gives the same result as multiplying by 1.

But Mrs Samuels had more to say about that question, and it was a bit obscure. She started telling us about something she called the "multiplicative identity." She said in every multiplication we really start from 1. Like, 2 times 3 is 1 times 2 times 3; 10 times 52 is 1 times 10 times 52. And so on. What makes 1 the "multiplicative identity" is that when you multiply any number by 1, you just get that number. OK. (And zero is the additive identity. When you add zero to any number, you just get that number. OK.)

When you have 2 raised to the zero, it's not just writing 2 zero times, which wouldn't give you anything; because you start with 1, which is the multiplicative identity, 1, and you write 2 zero times, and so you get 1. See? Any number raised to the power zero has got to be equal to 1. It can't be zero after all, whatever you might think at first.

Well, this was pretty easy to understand. Some people

griped about the answers but I thought they were fine. It was clear, crystal clear. Rob didn't get it – of course. I kept trying to explain it to him and then finally I gave up and said, "Look, it's right, believe me, memorize it. You'll get a better mark on the exam." So he did.

So we're going along, and it's getting to spring in our last year of high school. I am sailing through math, getting the best marks in the class and loving it, really loving it, because it all works out so nice and it's so easy. Then it starts to hit me.

It began with square roots. The square root of a number is a number which, multiplied by itself, gives you the first number. The square root of 4 is 2, since 2 times 2 is 4. But really 4 has two square roots, plus 2 and minus 2. A minus times a minus gives a plus, so minus 2 times minus 2 gives you 4. When we say things like the square root of 225 is 15, we are a bit off, because really it's plus or minus 15.

Well, somebody asks Mrs. Samuels whether every number has a square root and she says yes. Rob gets his hand in the air right away and asks what's the square root of minus 6. Wouldn't you know it?

Well, Mrs. Samuels had the answer, of course. She says right off, root-6 i. But nobody knows what that means, so she has to explain what i is. And that was the start of my problems.

This 'i', now, it's a number, a number *defined into existence*, Mrs. Samuels says, to represent the square root of minus one. So 'i', then, is a number which, when multiplied by itself, gives minus one. But 'i' is not a positive number or a negative number or zero. It can't be any of these, since positive numbers and negative numbers, squared, both give a positive answer, and zero squared just gives you zero. So 'i' is the square root of minus one, because that's how it's defined. But what sort of number is it?

I wasn't going to admit it, but I was kind of feeling with

Rob on this one. You just had to accept it, I guess. What really got me was the name for all this. Mrs. Samuels said numbers which can only be expressed using this 'i' are called *imaginary* numbers! I could just hear what Rob was going to say about that. Apparently, mathematics works perfectly well with these imaginary numbers, and somehow or other, they are even useful in electrical engineering, or so she said. They are called imaginary, but they aren't like fairy tales or whatever, because there are whole branches of mathematics about them, taught at universities and so on. It was hard to believe.

As if this wasn't bad enough, the next topic she had was infinity. Just an introduction, she said. I don't know why she had to get into all this strange stuff, especially at the end of the year with finals coming up and so on. She got started by telling this story about an infinite hotel. It has a guest in every room — meaning that it contains an infinite number of guests. Rob wondered if any of them were sleeping with each other in the same room, and if that would affect the math, but Mrs. Samuels said that wasn't the point.

Anyway, you have this hotel with an infinite number of rooms, and there is a guest in each room, an infinite number of guests. Then some more people show up, needing a room. Say there are 20 more. Even though there is a guest in every room, you can still fit them in, and without any doubling up. You move the guest in the first room into the 21st room, the guest in the second room into the 22nd room, and so on. You keep doing this, moving everybody, and you can get away with it, because it is an infinite hotel. The number of rooms is infinite, so at the end of it you can always go on. Everybody will get a room. Maybe nobody gets any sleep because they all have to move (ha ha) but then that doesn't affect the mathematics of infinity. Since the number of rooms is infinite, you can get more whenever you want.

Now 20 plus 100 gives a different number, but 20 plus

infinity is still infinity. That was supposed to be the point of this whole story about the hotel. Infinity doesn't behave like other numbers. It's special. You don't always just leave things undefined for infinity either, she said, because there are branches of math that deal with it, and there are special rules and so on.

In fact, there are even different kinds of infinity. There is an infinite number of different kinds of infinity! Good grief! But we weren't going to get into *that*.

I was getting fed up with this airy-fairy stuff, but Rob kind of liked it. He was cheerful about it, maybe because he suspected that I was suffering, for once. And it fit his idea that math was invented. But of course it wasn't, even though

I have to admit it was starting to make me nervous how often we were being told that things were just "defined" as this or that, or were not "defined." It could give you the wrong idea.

And some of this new stuff did seem pretty unrealistic. I mean, positive and negative numbers and triangles and zero were OK. But infinity? Worse yet, infinite numbers of different infinities? I couldn't swallow this business.

Finally, I decided to ask Mrs. Samuels about our argument. So I stayed after class to ask her: is math about the real world, or is it something people have just invented? I felt pretty stupid. Imagine asking a teacher whether she is teaching you about the real world! I mean, what other kind of world would anybody talk about? But anyway, she got us into all this, with her talk about imaginary numbers and the infinite hotel, and an infinity of infinities.

I didn't get the answer I wanted. She looked at me as if to say, "Now aren't you cute!", and she said it was great that Rob and I were arguing about some of the oldest questions in the philosophy of mathematics.

Philosophy of mathematics! That was the pits. I mean, what does a vague subject like philosophy have to do with math? Mrs. Samuels pulls out this book called *The Philosophy of Number* and says we should read it and talk about it, and it would give us a good basis for our "discussions."

Was that book weird! You wouldn't believe it. I suppose it must have been accurate enough, I mean, when it was just explaining what all these old guys thought about numbers long ago. But some of the ideas these people had! There was a fellow called Pythagoras. Actually, he was the one who proved the Pythagorean Theorem, you know, about how the square of the hypotenuse of a right-angled triangle equals the sum of the square on the other two sides. That's OK, of course, it's a good proof and it makes sense. But this same guy actually had a strange religion based on numbers.

People even thought he had performed miracles. He even thought things were made of numbers, arranged in various shapes to give different objects. Just to show you how crazy it was, the religion also said you couldn't eat beans. Well, Pythagoras lived around five hundred years B.C. so I guess you can't expect too much.

But that was just the beginning. Take Plato, a couple of centuries later. He thought that numbers and things like triangles and circles, and even equality, existed as Timeless Forms in some special kind of heaven, and that people learned math there before they were even born. Then when we learn math here on earth, it seems natural and logical because we already knew it once before. Maybe Rob missed out on his heaven, and that's why he never could do math. (Ha ha!) Plato thought math was solid and reliable and because the real world changes all the time, math has to be about objects in another world that doesn't change. Get that! And this guy is famous, I mean he wrote lots of stuff people are still studying today, all over the world.

According to this book, these Greeks thought knowledge had to be about things that never changed. They really liked math, because there was one right answer you could know for sure. I could see that. They liked things to be rational. When they found out that the square root of two doesn't work out to any number with a simple fraction, they were just shocked. It isn't a rational number, because when you work it out, the decimal goes on forever. People nearly committed suicide over this!

You would think things would get better when history progressed to—you know, after the Middle Ages. They did in a way. Descartes discovered those Cartesian coordinate axes, the x and y axis, we call them, where you can draw algebra equations, so you can kind of bring algebra and geometry together. Then there was Leibniz, who discovered calculus. Along with Newton, the book said, and then they argued about who was first. But anyway. With this calculus, you can handle really small things, so small they are just about nothing. Infinitesimals. Even though they are too small to really exist, you can use calculus to sum them up. And you need to do this to do physics. I didn't quite get it, but it sounded neat.

But still, strange things were going on. Like this Berkeley, who was a philosopher and an Irish bishop. He believed that all our ideas come from sensation. That makes sense, I think. I mean, things are out there, and we find out by looking and touching and hearing and so on — having sensations. Experiences. Only Berkeley just took it too far. He said that if you didn't have a sensation relating to something, you couldn't have an idea of it either. He applied this to math, and he said there was no such thing as one ten thousandth of an inch. Because you couldn't experience it, it didn't exist. Then he got in trouble with physics. It needed calculus and infinitesimals, which he said were illusions.

Then there was Kant. He was kind of like Plato. Only he lived in Germany around the time of the French Revolution, and being more modern, he didn't say numbers were up in heaven. He said we had special things in our minds, I think he called them intuitions. And math is the same for everybody because we all make it up according to the way our minds are made up, and all our minds are made up the same way. We have this kind of framework of intuitions in our brains, and we construct these mathematical things, like the number five and triangles and infinity.

Kant was big on Euclid's geometry, apparently. He thought you could prove it was true, and it was the basis of all science.

Well, that's obvious, isn't it? But you know what? In this book, the author said this was Kant's well-known "mistake," to assume that Euclid's geometry was absolutely true and was about the world. I was so bugged by this, I even checked his footnotes. And he talked about the "well-known fact" that there are geometries different from Euclid's. In some, triangles have angles that add up to less than 180 degrees and some, more. Can you imagine? Rob, of course, said he could imagine it. But I couldn't.

The worst of it was, whenever I came to something that seemed sensible and right, it was immediately followed by something crazy. Like the bit about the one ten thousandth of an inch. Or else the author would immediately say it was "obviously false" or "quite certainly incorrect" or something. It really got to me.

I could have known. It was right there in the author's introduction, only Rob was so keen to read the book that we had skipped that part. Right there, right at the beginning, he started to say this completely sensible stuff. You know, what anyone would think, like math is about things in the world and it's the study of their actual relations of quantity, to find out how they work and so on. Yeah, I know it sounds boring, but at least it makes sense, right? But this author calls these ideas "naive empiricism", and he says they are "universally regarded as incorrect today." Incorrect! Those ideas were my ideas, and I was always real good at math. Then he says understanding that these are incorrect is "preliminary" to understanding the real nature of mathematics.

OK, OK. So I had to go on reading this. *Why* were these ideas so wrong? He said it was because they could not explain why mathematics was necessarily true and they could not explain how it was independent of what we actually experience. And because so many things in mathematics, like infinities and infinitesimals and imaginary numbers, are not things in the real world. Well, I could buy that last point. By "necessary", he meant it has to be that way. When you add 5 and 7 the right answer is 12; they have to sum to 12, not anything else, or you have a contradiction. This "have to" means it's "necessary" and you can't get it from experiencing the world, because experience only tells you how things *are*. It doesn't tell you how they *must* be.

Numbers aren't really in things, he said. They aren't properties of things. The number system is something "a priori," independent of experience, and we use it to organize what we experience.

You don't experience zero, or a mathematical point, or a straight line, or a perfect circle, or even equality. Much less an infinitesimal or the square root of minus one. Strictly speaking, you don't even experience the number five. (You can imagine how Rob was gloating over that one.) I didn't really want to accept this stuff. I didn't like it at all. But it was hard to argue against it. I mean, who *has* experienced exact equality, or a perfect circle? Or infinity?

Given that this empiricism was wrong, then what was mathematics about anyway? This author said there were three important modern theories and he tried to explain what they were. But to me they all sounded just about the same. Anyway, they all made math something people *invent* – just the way Rob had said it was, way back when. I can't remember what these theories were called, but to me none of them were based on common sense, not at all.

But the clincher was still to come. This author said that underneath all of mathematics there is still a "profound mystery". Yeah, that's how he put it, a profound mystery. The mystery is that these invented systems of number and all these fancy concepts apply to the real world. They are useful in just thousands of ways for science, engineering, banking, and all kinds of other things. But according to him, nobody has ever really been able to explain how and why systems we just invent can work so well. *Why* should something we make up help us predict and control the real world, which we don't make up? This is the "mystery". In fact, the author got so carried away, going on about this, that he even said mathematical systems were "almost magical" in their powers.

That was it. I just didn't feel like reading any more. The book wasn't going to be on the exam, and I never liked math for its profound mysteries. I liked things that were clear and neat and made sense, like math used to.

I aced the final, of course. There weren't any questions about imaginary numbers or the infinite hotel. It was like before. But it didn't feel the same. I had lost that old idea that it was all clear-cut and I understood everything.

You can bet I wasn't going to seek a future inventing intellectual objects or thinking about profound mysteries or magical powers. Not this man. Reading that book put an end to my brilliant mathematical career.

I went into computer engineering. It's going pretty well.

As for Rob, he went off and studied philosophy, he liked reading and arguing about that book so much. He seems to be happy enough. But I ask you, is he really going anywhere? I asked him once and you know what he said? "Where are people supposed to be going?" Can you beat that?

WHAT MAKES SELVES?

Robin: Jan, I found some old pictures today. There was one of you when you were only about three, running across the beach with a sandpail. Want to see it?

Jan: Sure, I guess so.

Robin: Here. I really like the way your hair is blowing across your face and the innocent look in your eyes, gazing straight out at the camera.

Jan: But Robin, I don't think that's me. I was never like that.

Chris: It's got to be you Jan, it's marked on the back. You were just too young to remember. If you asked your parents, they could tell you where you were and what was going on.

Jan: The photo seems kind of unreal. I can't connect myself with that cute little thing.

Chris: Use your common sense, Jan. It's a family shot, and it has "Jan, 3 years, 1969," written right on it. I mean, what more do you need?

Robin: I think I know what you mean, Jan. The other night when I was watching TV a life insurance salesman came around and tried to sell me a policy which would give me a nice little pension in the year 2035. Can you imagine?

Jan: What's the problem — imagining the year 2035, or imagining yourself 50 years older than you are now, or what?

Robin: Both, I guess.

Chris: Let's see, in 2035, you'd be 69. Right? That's not so very old.

Robin: I call it old.

Jan: So did you buy the life insurance?

Robin: I couldn't really afford it, so I didn't have to decide. It does make you think, though. I kept trying to imagine being a 69 year old person in 2035, and I just couldn't do it. I can't make any connection between me and some little old person way in the future.

Jan: Just the way I can't make any connection with that little person on the beach.

Robin: What makes that little kid and you one and the same person? I mean, why is it *you*? Not just because your mother says so! And how can somebody forty or fifty years from now still be me?

Chris: I don't think there's any real problem. You keep your identity even though you change. When you grow an inch, you change. Or when you dye your hair blond or purple, or pierce your ears, or gain forty pounds, or even shave your head. But none of these changes mean you stop being you. You're the same human being. If anybody wanted to, they could trace your body right through your whole life, from one place to another. It would have one single path through space, with no breaks, whether you dyed your hair purple, or gained weight, or whatever.

Jan: If I paint my house, it's still the same house. It just has a different color.

Robin: But aren't there limits to the kinds of changes you can have and still be the same person? Suppose I suddenly became 12 feet tall? Or, in a whizz bang feat of brainpower, got a perfect grasp of Chinese and was whisked away to run a huge factory in some place like Shanghai. Would I still be me?

Chris: For heaven's sake, Robin! You learn gradually, just the way you grow gradually. A person is a human being who's first an infant, then a toddler, a child, teenager, adult, middle-aged person, old person, and so on, because that is the life cycle for human beings. You learn and you change, maybe even quite a bit, and of course you get older. But you're still the same person through it all.

Robin: The final change is, you're dead. Are you the same person right through this too?

Chris: Gosh, I don't know. But that's a whole other problem, Robin. Stick to the point.

Jan: Chris, I think you're being too physical about this whole thing. You're looking at people like purely physical things, as if we were just animals. We're born, we grow, we change. We live, we die. So what?

Chris: Human beings are animals.

Robin: Not just animals. We human beings have souls.

Chris: Souls? Come on.

Jan: If you don't like souls, say minds.

Robin: Or selves. 'Minds' sounds just intellectual. What we were talking about is being a self, being a person. Me being *myself* now and wondering whether I could still be myself in 2035, and you being *yourself* now and wondering whether you were that little person in the picture from 1969. Being a person isn't just having a human body, and being the same person in the past and future isn't just having the same body that grows from a baby to an adult. It's your self that matters.

Jan: That's it, Chris. Each of us is ourself, and what puzzles Robin and me is how we can be the same self as somebody at a past time we can't remember or a future time we can't even imagine.

Chris: 'Each of us is ourself'? Jan, you are starting to sound like an idiot. The way I see it, both of you are making a big fuss about nothing. We are human beings and we have brains. These brains make us able to see and hear and feel things and think about the world and each other. When we become aware of things, we think, and we get a sense of ourselves. So, each of us thinks he is a self. But so what? There isn't any deep mystery about it. It's the *brain* that makes you yourself. If your brain lasts 70 years, your self does too. Sure, it changes when you grow and learn more, and so on, and you change too, but you are still the same person through all of it.

Robin: Chris, I know we have brains. That's not the point. It's more a psychological thing, how you feel the same person at these far-removed times. Someday I'll be old. I know that. But how will that old person be *me*, when I *now* am me, and I can't make any connection?

Chris: You just don't have enough imagination. If it's *your* brain in *your* body, it will be *you*.

Robin: You think people are just brains in bodies, and you say I don't have imagination? What is this?

Jan: Come on, guys, don't fight. You know, this business of your self and your body reminds me of a conversation I once had with a friend of my mother's. She said that when you're middle aged or old, you never really get used to it. You still think of yourself as you were when you were in your prime — in your early twenties. When you look in the mirror and see wrinkles, grey hair, and a double chin, you don't think you're seeing yourself. Not your real self.

Chris: Of course the advertising industry doesn't help much, showing pictures where people are always slim and young and perfect looking. It's too bad people identify so much with their bodies and not more with their real self, in the brain.

Robin: Chris, your brain is part of your body. What's this distinction you're suddenly making between the brain and the body? But anyway, are you starting to understand the problem?

Chris: The *self* is no more a separate thing than the *will*. I think a person is an animal, a higher animal. People are conscious because they have brains, and because they have quite complicated brains, they are even conscious that they are conscious. I mean, they are aware of things and they know they are aware of things. It is the brain that does all this. It processes perceptions and it is so complex it even lets us know that we know things about the world.

Robin: Your brain is part of your body. It's not your real

self.

Jan: Didn't someone once compare the self to an onion?

Chris: Oh that's helpful, Jan. Great. Maybe I'll go look in the fridge and see if I can find my real self there.

Jan: It's a comparison, Chris. For Pete's sake. When you talk about the brain letting you know, and then letting you know that you know, it makes me think it could go on and on. The onion has layers that go on and on.

Robin: It was Ibsen who said that about the onion. It's in his play *Peer Gynt*. But I don't think he was talking about knowing and knowing that you know and knowing that you know that you know and that whole thing. It was the difficulty in getting to the real inner self. Your *true self*. When you think you know yourself, you might still be looking at something in a kind of disguise. You might not have the real core self. You can have the same brain in the same body without having the sense that you are the same self. Just the way with an onion; you think you have got to the center but there always seems to be another layer that can be peeled off.

Chris: You two make everything so complicated. We are what we are because of the way our brains are. Because our brains let us know and let us be aware of knowing, we have a sense of self. As long as you hang on to your brain, you'll be yourself. It's *that* simple.

Robin: I'm not so sure.

Jan: You hear about the true self and the real self and

so on because it's so hard to find out what the self really is.

Robin: What if I had a heart attack and my brain was quickly removed from my head and supported in a bottle by an artificial system that kept it alive? Would that brain in a bottle be *me*?

Chris: Robin, what do I have to do to make you come down to earth? Yes, it might be you, if the supports for the brain were good enough, and if that part of the brain that makes you aware of things still worked. But it's not going to happen, so you don't have to worry about it.

Robin: In principle, though, you think I could become a brain in a bottle? And it would still be me?

Chris: Of course you'd look different to others, very different, and you might not be able to communicate. You couldn't talk because you wouldn't have a mouth or any vocal chords.

Jan: It sounds gruesome. Thank goodness scientists haven't started doing that yet!

Robin: Don't be too sure.

Chris: Look, all I want to say is that a normal person has a body and a brain and a sense of self and a personality. And as long as his brain holds together, he will be himself. It's really quite simple!

Jan: I'm not sure it's that easy, Chris. It's not that Robin and I think the *self* is a kind of ghost inside the body, floating around somewhere inside the skull. It's that our sense of *self* is not a sense of what the *brain* is. It's *my* brain. I'm not my brain.

Chris: Oh, come on. You say "myself," but that doesn't mean there is a "my," over and above the self. That wouldn't make sense!

Robin: Having one self isn't just a matter of having one brain, because sometimes there are several selves in a single body. Did you ever read any of those books about people with split personalities?

Jan: You mean like Dr. Jekyll and Mr. Hyde?

Robin: Yes. But that was just a story, not really true. The ones I was thinking of were *The Three Faces Of Eve* and *Sybil*. Eve was a woman about thirty years ago who had three really different personalities. The selves were so separate from each other that one would do something another wouldn't even remember. Eve White was a drab housewife and Eve Black, another self based in the same body, was a glamorous type who went off to wild parties in low cut dresses and so on. Eve Black would do these things Eve White didn't know how to do and couldn't even remember.

Chris: How did they know she wasn't a fake? If you had to lead a dull housewife's life, it would be neat to pretend to have one or two extra selves. These extra selves could go off and live it up, and then you could pretend not to know anything about it. You could get away with some pretty wild things.

Jan: I can't remember exactly, Chris, but this Eve White did seek help. Her case was studied, and she was eventually cured by a psychiatrist. It's a really famous case. There was even a movie about it, called *The Three Faces of Eve*.

Chris: It sounds as though this Eve was really out of her mind.

Jan: Whatever *that* means.

Chris: Come on, Jan. Don't bug me. So was Eve ever cured?

Robin: A fourth personality, Jane, emerged. She was able to kind of combine some key features of the other three. By the way, Jane divorced Eve White's husband. I guess she couldn't stand Eve's boring life.

Chris: Boy, I don't know. It sounds like faking to me. Were there really three or four selves? Or was there just one, deliberately forgetting information and impressing the doctors?

Jan: It's hard to say for sure. But the fact that it's even possible shows that the self or personality is not the very same as the brain. The personality can't be just a matter of how the brain and body are, because there could be different personalities in the same brain.

Chris: Personalities are *in* the brain? Where? What parts?

Jan: Don't be so picky, Chris. Not really in it — associated with it. You know what I mean.

Robin: Sybil was even more dramatic than Eve, because she had sixteen different personalities.

Chris: That's crazy!

Robin: Just listen. Most of these personalities were female, but some were male. They all had different memories, different ways of talking, different interests, and even different skills. One of the male selves was good at carpentry, but none of the others could do it at all. Sybil really needed help, because she was always switching from self to self. It was actually dangerous. One self would travel, say from New York to Philadelphia, and then another self would wake up in Philadelphia not knowing where it was.

Jan: Good grief! You mean she would wake up and not know what city she was in, or how she got there?

Robin: Right. Eventually her psychiatrist discovered that all these different selves had started because Sybil's mother had really mistreated her when she was small. She was very cruel, and Sybil handled it by setting up a separate self that hadn't suffered and didn't remember the terrible things. The whole process of splitting the self started there, and then it just kept happening again and again.

Jan: That's awful. And sixteen selves—what a mess! Was she ever cured?

Robin: I think so. I think it was her psychiatrist who wrote the book.

Chris: These cases are so weird. They aren't normal people like us. We have normal working brains and one self each. I mean, these are rare cases. I'll bet there aren't many scientists who believe in three or four selves in one body. Much less sixteen!

Jan: Actually, even normal people have more than one self.

Chris: Don't be ridiculous.

Jan: Seriously. Haven't you heard of the left brain and the right brain? You know, how they are supposed to have very different functions and thinking styles? In most right-handed people, it is the left brain that is more logical and more precise with words and so on, and the right brain that is more intuitive and imaginative, and better at relating things in space.

Chris: So?

Jan: Well there are some operations, mainly for epilepsy patients, I think, where the connecting tissue between these two sides of the brain is cut. Then you get weird things. If something is shown only to the left eye, for instance, the person may be able to hold it with his left hand but not say what it is, you know, because his right eye, which is connected up with the more verbal part of the brain, doesn't see it.

Chris: But how would that show he has two selves?

Jan: One side of his brain is aware of the thing and the other side isn't. His consciousness is split. His thinking is divided, you know, in two parts. It is the self that thinks. So you could say he has two selves.

Robin: So are we all really two selves? One for the right brain, our imaginative mystical self, and one for the left brain, our thinking talking logical self? When we say, "I'm of two minds about that," maybe we really mean it!

Jan: You could say that. In most people these two sides

of the brain are very different. So we could say that in most of us two selves exist at the same time, in one body.

Chris: That's not right, Jan. They have to set up special experiments to prevent the information from getting to the other side of the brain. They have to rig things up. Even people who have these unusual operations don't usually see only through the left eye. Things are coordinated. And in normal people, the two sides of the brain can communicate. Information gets transferred from one side to the other. It is put together and made into a whole. There is one personality with one set of skills, memories, and so on. Just because there are some odd cases after an operation doesn't mean everybody is really two selves. For Pete's sake!

Robin: Pete? Who's Pete, your other self?

Jan: I just had a thought.

Chris: Did you do it yourself or was it a group effort?

Jan: Don't be so smart. You know, it just occurred to me. We've been thinking of these strange cases where people have more selves than usual. Eve had three, then four, before she was settled into one. Sybil had sixteen. These epilepsy patients might have two. Maybe other people have two, if their brain hemispheres are really different from each other, and if they somehow get separated so the normal communication is not there. But does anybody have *less* than normal?

Chris: Normal is one. One self per brain. That is a

Robin:	normal brain, in a normal person. So less than one is zero.
Robin:	Brilliant. Did you do that calculation all by yourself?
Chris:	Actually, no. It took three selves, or three of me, that is — one to get the information, another to think "so", and a third to conclude that the answer is zero.
Jan:	Don't be silly.
Chris:	You think that everyone might have two selves, and you accuse *me* of being silly?
Jan:	Robin, listen. This business of zero selves might be important. If there are human beings with brains and with no sense of self, then doesn't that prove that the sense of self is something extra, not just the purely physical human being?
Chris:	Well, there are human beings without any sense of self. Really small babies, I suppose. But adults? I don't know.
Chris:	Now that you mention it, I think I remember seeing something about that in that book by Oliver Sacks. You know, the one with the amazing title?
Robin:	You mean *The Man Who Mistook His Wife For A Hat*?
Chris:	That's it. There were a couple of people described in there who had really terrible memory problems. If I remember it right, Sacks even wondered whether they had a sense of who they were at all.
Jan:	You mean they couldn't remember their pasts?

Chris: One of them, I think Sacks called him Jimmy, could remember his past quite well, but only until 1945. After that he had no memory at all. But what really made Jimmy puzzling was that he had just about no short term memory. I mean, if Sacks talked with him, even for quite a while, and then went away for five minutes, he would act as if he had never met Sacks ever before. He was smart and could do math problems and so on, but only if they were very short. Otherwise he would forget the beginning of the problem before he got to the end. He couldn't link his ideas at 10 o'clock to his ideas at five minutes after 10. Really! But he could remember lots of things from the second world war.

Robin: What about the other case?

Chris: That was a man too. William, I think Sacks called him. His short term memory was even worse than Jimmy's and he didn't have any long term memory either. What he did was talk constantly, making up stories about what was going on and where he fitted in. There wasn't really anything to him, just these great tales coming out. If he stopped talking, he just wouldn't *be* as a person.

Jan: That sounds even worse.

Chris: That's what Sacks thought. Apparently with Jimmy, there were certain things that suggested he was aware of himself in some ways. For instance, he could recognize his brother, even though he remembered him the way he had looked in 1945 and was always amazed at how old he looked. Also, he seemed to be calm and present during church services. Because he had his memories from before 1945, you could get a sense of the sort of young man he had been.

Robin: And then, because they were *his* memories, you could think he was still that person, so you would say he had a self.

Jan: Or he *was* a self.

Chris: Right. But you know you can't really get a relationship with somebody whose short term memory is less than 5 minutes. You're too limited in how you can get together. I mean, you talk about the same subjects over and over again and there is no thread, no connection.

Robin: Jimmy was hardly a person anymore, with so little of his short-term memory left.

Jan: So what about William?

Chris: What made William worse was that he didn't have any past he could remember either. He told stories about the past all the time, but he kept changing them. He was always making different things up, and the stories were quite funny, but they kept shifting. You just got the idea there was nothing to him except all those unreliable inventions.

Robin: But Sacks is a doctor. He didn't say William had no self, did he? I mean, what a thing for a doctor to say about his patient!

Jan: I'm just thinking about that expression my Dad always used to use. "Pull yourself together," he'd say. Maybe this means more than you'd think.

Chris: What do you mean?

Jan: It almost seems as though a person has a self or is a self because he or she makes one.

Robin: You create *yourself*? How could you do that?

Jan: You're a self because you connect things you remember and experience. That's what makes you a person, more than a physical being. I find it hard to believe I was ever three because I can't connect me now with somebody who's only three. We find it hard to think of what we'll be like in forty or fifty years because we can't connect ourselves with old people. And it's hard to understand how William or Jimmy can be selves because they can't connect ideas and conversations over even really short periods of time. If somebody can't connect what's happening now to what happened five minutes ago, there is hardly anyone there at all. Nobody we can relate to, anyway.

Robin: Except by relating to other connections, like with the more distant past. Provided these still exist.

Chris: Do you mean that if there are no connections between experiences at different times, there is just no self?

Jan: Something like that, I guess. We have to link things. Thinking back to connecting this stuff with that picture of me and Robin's ideas about life insurance, I think what bothered us was that we couldn't make any connection with those other selves. I couldn't imagine the child on the beach being me, because I couldn't connect *me* now with that scene, and I couldn't relate any experience I had then to what I experience and remember now. Maybe I just lack imagination, I don't know. But

I can't remember it. I can't imagine at all what it is like to experience the world as a three or four year old.

Robin: That's it. I can't connect with a 69 year old person in 2035, so I have trouble thinking I would ever be such a person.

Chris: Actually, when you think about it, we have to make connections, just to experience things in the present.

Robin: Music, for instance. You're right. When you hear a tune, you are remembering the notes before the ones you hear, and looking forward to the notes to come. If you didn't do that, you couldn't hear a melody at all.

Jan: It's the same for understanding sentences. You have to remember the beginning, and connect it to the end.

Robin: We do hear melodies, practically everybody does. We connect things from different things from different times just to be conscious at all. But people like Jimmy and William can just barely do it, not enough for even the present moment to make much sense to them.

Chris: This business about selves depending on connected experiences still sounds wired to me. Wouldn't it be better just to talk about people as human beings pure and simple.

Jan: Chris, you just don't seem to be interested in personalities. Look, when people make all these connections, what makes for personality is that different people make different connections.

Robin: How do you mean?

Jan: Well, they have different experiences in the first place and then they select different ones to remember, and think about them differently and so on.

Robin: Isn't that part of what makes one person different from another? Things are related and organized for everybody but in different ways? The connections not only make a person himself, but they make different people different selves.

Jan: It's a bit like countries. You can ask what makes Britain today the same country as Britain in 1500, and there will be an answer in terms of history, the connections between different kings and queens, Parliament, properties, laws, and so on. All those connections make Britain the same country as in 1500.

Robin: Despite all the changes?

Jan: I think so. It can be the same country even though there have been huge changes, like Britain becoming an imperial power with a vast colonial empire, and then losing the empire, all sorts of things. But Britain now and Britain in 1500 are the same country, even though it is different in many ways.

Chris: Just the way you are the same person as that little kid on the beach, even though you have changed so much since then.

Jan: I guess so — if I really *am*.

Chris: If you want to think about Britain and its identity, you could also ask what makes Britain today different from another country today. Say France.

Jan: Right. And there too you would talk about connections. Things would fit together into one kind of pattern in Britain, and another kind in France?

Chris: Something like that.

Robin: Is the idea supposed to be that just as the type of connections make Britain distinct from France, the type of connections make me different from you, Jan?

Jan: That's about it. I mean, every self can only last through time because it connects experiences at different times, mostly through memory. But also, different selves have different styles and personalities. Part of what makes them so different is the different associations and connections they make.

Chris: Like memories, you mean?

Jan: Of course. Memories are the main connection. They link us with our earlier selves and they also make us different from each other. I don't remember what you experienced. But associations matter too. You know, one person might associate the town of Peterborough, Ontario with a houseboat trip because he had first heard of it when trying to rent a houseboat. Another might associate it with trucks, because he knew about the major truck manufacturer in Peterborough, England.

Chris: Yes, but I can't see why that's so important. Peterborough and other towns are what they are, regardless of what different emotions and ideas people may have about them.

Jan: One or two associations may seem unimportant, but people have billions and trillions of experiences during life. Everyone's are so different, and then they select different ones to remember and reflect on them and connect them in such different ways. That's what makes personalities so different.

Chris: To me this sounds complicated and fuzzy-headed. If we ask what makes me me and you you, the answer is easy. I'm here with my body and brain, and you're over there with yours. Our bodies are easy to tell apart, and our brains probably would be too, if somebody who knew a lot could look closely at them.

Jan: For once and for all, Chris, it's the self, personality, I'm talking about, not just the body and brain. I'm trying to say that all the really different memories and connections and associations people have help to define their different personalities. These aren't all there is to a person, of course, not even all there is to personality. Physical appearance has a big effect on the experiences we have.

Robin: I'll always remember a teacher I had when I was thirteen. She had to teach sex education, which was kind of funny, because she was middle-aged and dowdy and sort of puritanical in style. Well, one day she was telling us how she had not had sex before she was married, and didn't find that very hard, but maybe, she said, that was because nobody had tried very hard to talk her into it. I thought it was so frank for her to tell us that, and

I'll always remember the way she got so personal, though she usually seemed like such an old-fashioned type.

Jan: That's a perfect example of what I mean.

Chris: You mean that physical appearance has an effect on your personality by affecting what experiences you have?

Jan: That too, but more. You see, the minute I said that, Robin remembered something quite unique, this teacher and this confession in the class.

Chris: Well, presumably Robin wasn't the only student there. Others could remember it too.

Jan: Sure, of course, but the thing is, for Robin this experience was really important, and it's the thing she remembers most about that teacher and that class.

Chris: Others might do that too.

Jan: OK, they might, but they still don't have all Robin's other memories and associations. It's Robin who's here now, and she's connecting just that experience with that teacher and our arguments about personal identity. Nobody else has done just that. Robin is unique, with just these memories and making just these connections.

Chris: So are you saying that connections between experiences make selves? Because we can connect experiences over shorter and longer times, mainly by remembering them, we can be people with a past, present, and future. And because people have different experiences, with different memories and associations, there are distinct personalities, distinct selves. It's not the body or the brain, but the way all these experiences are linked together?

Jan: I think that's more or less it. In most of us there is one kind of system or organization, relating all these experiences. But in some peculiar cases, like Eve and Sybil, things go wrong, and there are several systems that aren't connected to each other. That's how several selves can exist with in one body.

Chris: I don't think those multiple personalities were ever real in the first place.

Jan: It's pretty abnormal, but it would be possible. And that's the point. It's the pattern of experiences that makes a human being the person he is, or the person she is, and if the experiences are related and connected abnormally, in distinct groups, then you could have different persons associated with the very same body and brain. One self is one set of experiences connected by memory and other things.

Robin: But it can't be as simple as *that*. The self *can't* just be a matter of having connected experiences.

Jan: Why not? It makes sense to me.

Robin: Something has to connect them! I mean, if one experience gets connected to another experience, then there is something or someone doing the connecting. *That* must be the self. I remember my teacher, and I make the association between what she said and what you are saying about the relation between body and personality. It isn't that myself is a whole bundle of connected experiences. It is myself, me. I, Robin, make these connections.

Chris: Are you trying to say connecting doesn't just happen, something has to do it?

Robin: Yes. And that something is the self.

Chris: So the self can't just be a bundle of connected experiences?

Robin: Right. Because it is the self that has those experiences, and remembers them, and connects them.

Jan: I'm not sure. It's natural to talk that way, but you seem to be making the self into some kind of thing. A *self*, that sits inside your skull making connections. A little Robin inside, to create the connections that make personality for the big Robin we know and love!

Robin: Jan, don't be so mean. I'm serious. Really! There has to be some kind of self to make the connections. It's just basic logic. The reason it's natural to talk that way is because it's *true*. One of my experiences doesn't associate with another one, all by itself. I can't be just a collection of all these memories and experiences and stuff, because I have to be the thing that collects them. That's myself.

Chris: I don't think this is a real problem. Of course there is something making the connections. It's the brain. The brain is so complicated that it can be aware of being aware, and it has storage for billions of experiences. There are nerves and neurons, and axons, and dendrites, all that sort of stuff. And that's how it happens. If we are going to understand how experiences are remembered and connected, we have to understand how the *brain* works. There must be a kind of system in the brain, that organizes all these things and makes it possible for us to be selves.

Robin: It's so hard to understand.

Jan: Maybe that's because we have to use our brain to try to understand our brain.

Chris: I can see that, as far as psychology goes, what makes selves and personalities is memories and connections. A self has to be whole, or mostly whole, and things have to be experienced and then related. But eventually all this has to be explained in terms of the brain.

Robin: So something does put all these things together.

Chris: Right. And that something is the brain. It must be the brain! It can't be a little man or woman or ghost or spirit called "Self" or "Mini-Robin", or whatever, sitting inside the skull.

Jan: Do you think scientists can explain how Eve got four selves and Sybil got sixteen, just in terms of the brain?

Chris: Not now, probably. But some day. Why not? Assuming, that is, that they really had these different selves, which I'm not sure is right in the first place. But if they did, then sure, there has to be something about their brains which would explain it. And if you could study their brains carefully enough, you would know how it happened.

Robin: You *could*, you say. But of course nobody does.

Chris: Well it's better than ghosts, isn't it?

Robin: I guess so, but only a little.

Jan: So we are persons because we connect and relate our experiences, and when we connect them, it's really our brains doing it?

Chris: Right.

Jan: Whatever 'really' means.

Chris: Jan, you always have to have the last word. That's enough. Let's go see a movie or something.

Robin: Maybe we can see *The Three Faces of Eve*. It's on with the fifties rerun series at the Plaza.

ROOMMATES IN SPACE

They say they put me in a hospital. For people sick in the head. There's yellow all around, dull yellow. Not sun. Am I in bed? Beds, hospitals, just figments, not substantial, not solid or real. I could move right through it all, right through that wall. Out. I could see everything from up there. Or from underneath, or inside. There is just empty space.

But I feel the sheet. It is grainy, kind of, stiff. Looks gray, not white. Sad. Feelings are real. People. People put me here. Mum and Dad. They said I couldn't float to the mountain-top, I couldn't see their bed from above. They think I'm crazy, I know, but they don't say it, not that. They say I can't go through things, because they just don't know how it is. Don't know things are empty. Nothing.

Can I turn my head? That thing they call my head? Blond; they say I'm pretty. But it's empty, no gray mush inside, no brain, what they think is me. I can move it. Then I see the other.

Hairs are brown, dull brown. And gray. She looks old, her head. Messy. Is she sick too? She's like my mother, but thinner. Not my mother, no. Does she know I can fly outside my body? I would get above her bed, around by the yellow door, on the other side. I'd be there, watching. Me. Not this empty body. Not the blond head. The real me could see everything she did. Any part of her. For her, a danger.

There is shaking. She's a gray lump, moving, gulping, choking. So why is she here?

Patient Report: Caitlin M. May 31, 1988.

*Age 16. Weight dangerously low. Near-anorexic.
Committed by parents. Has had out-of-body experiences. Won't accept reality of body. Deluded,
insists she can move through objects and "things are
empty", "nothing is solid". Refuses to walk or eat.
Weak from not eating, won't care for her body; insists
it's not her real self. Thoughts disordered. Speech
confused.*

J. Weinstein, Psychiatrist

Patient Report: Ellen T. May 31, 1988

*Age 43. Unmarried. Professor of Physics, Ontado
University. Voluntary patient. Exhaustion, extreme
depression, possibly from overwork. Borderline
paranoia, low confidence in others. Apparently
clear thinking, frequently insists science is a fraud
because people can't be trusted. Speech clear,
general health not bad.*

J. Weinstein, Psychiatrist

*Recommended treatment: Caitlin M. — High calorie
diet. Rest. Company of Ellen T, mature scientist,
will perhaps restore her common sense. (JW)*

*Recommended treatment: Ellen T. — Rest. Sym-
pathetic conversation. Company of Caitlin M, innocent younger person, will perhaps help to restore
her confidence in others. (JW)*

She's crying, really crying. Why? Tears are nothing, not water. Empty. Feelings real. Can I talk? Talk to her?

"Why are you crying? Who are you? Why are you here? Why are you crying?" I can't just listen to those choking noises, see that shaking lump of gray. Will she turn? Stringy hair, a thin face. A thin arm comes out from the sheets. Glasses. She takes kleenex to wipe her face, blow her nose. Then talk?

"Who are you? My god, you're young. Why did they put me here with someone so young?"

Angry? Doesn't like me. Who's too young—young is good. Talk more. She isn't crying now, not shaking. Looking. Looking at me. Tell her. "You're real. Something real, because you have feelings. They say I have a body, in a bed, in a hospital. Food. They say I need food. Steak, awful red stuff, bloody. Sticky oranges. Awful figments, but nothing real. There's only my mind. No body, I don't need food. Figments."

Now she looks at me, hard. Watery eyes, weak blue, dark lines under, halfway down her cheeks. Awful. Do I look so bad too? Don't care. Illusion, no matter. Stares at me. She's waking up. No more tears. Focused, focused on me.

"Beds and hospitals aren't real? Steak and oranges not solid things? My dear, you had better eat some breakfast when it comes. You're under-nourished, your thinking isn't clear. If steak isn't solid, I'm crazy."

"Crazy. That's a good one. Why we're here. My parents say I'm crazy. They don't believe I can fly. But I saw it, everything, right from the mountaintop. I was up there, above it all. Not my body, just me. I flew up there, my soul, I saw it all down below, my body too. Moved right through, through the walls, zipped over the town, to the top. No body. Things are nothing. No-things. I felt it."

Now she stares at me. She knows I'm real. She's real.

107

Can talk, doesn't cry now. Does she believe me?

"Interesting, very interesting. You're only the second one I've met, though I've read some articles on that, oh yes, yes, that book by Celia Green too. My dear, you had an out-of-body experience. They're quite well known, yes, quite well known. And it was wonderful. They always are. That sense of floating loose, of power."

"You know it? You believe me?" She knows I can fly? Not my mother, better. She's better than a mother. For right now.

"My dear, I believe you, of course. Of course you had the experience, you felt like you were flying, soaring, and you had the impression, the world perceived from high up."

"My body too. I was way above my body. Moved without my body. I'm not my body. I could see everything from the top of the mountain."

"Yes, and it felt beautiful. They all say that, I've heard. But you have to understand, the world doesn't stop because you had a beautiful experience. It's like kind of magic, I think. Everything seems so vivid, yes, I've read about this. But it's a sort of deception, a freak experience. You had a wonderful special experience, yes, I believe you. But things are still real. Beds and tables, yes, bodies, steaks, oranges, they don't lose their being just because something special has happened to you. If anything wasn't solid, it was your mind, not these objects."

"You know all this? Who are you? Did your daughter do it too? Did she fly? You know so much."

"I don't have a daughter, no. Not anyone. I'm alone."

Skinny fingers, tapping on the gritty sheets. No rings. How would she know it? Is she lecturing me? A teacher? "You a teacher, maybe?"

"Not exactly. Well, I do teach, but students older than you. I'm a professor at Ontado University. You know where it is? Not so far from here. I teach physics, well, microphysics, really."

That's scary. They put me in here with a physics professor? And I thought she was kind of like somebody's mother. But no, no children she said. Lectures? Is she here to teach me science? The hard facts? Show how things like steak and beds are all very real and sensible, not just feeling? She sits up, pulls her skinny fingers through her stringy hair. Her skins sags a bit under the chin. Like my mother's.

"You're a professor? For real?"

"For what it's worth, I've been a professor for fifteen years. I teach, I do research, in microphysics. Or I did. That's it. I used to do research."

More kleenex, glasses off, eyes wiped. She's crying again. Microphysics research. I hardly know what it is, and it's making her cry. Weird. She's not here for me. For her, herself. Crazy. Is she crazy? Can teachers go crazy too? Even them?

"What's microphysics research? Why does it make you cry?"

"Microphysics — the study of the nature and behaviour of the most elementary particles of things. Molecules, then atoms, electrons, neutrons, quarks, charmed particles, strange particles, all that."

"*That* makes you cry? Weird."

"Not that, my dear, not that. It's a wonder, a miracle, that it's comprehensible at all. All things made of particles that aren't parts at all. Smallest parts that aren't parts. The world is so much stranger than we think. You know what Einstein said? I think it's so beautiful. The most incomprehensible thing about the world is that it's comprehensible. Microphysics shows that, in every way it could."

"I don't understand. You don't make sense."

"Things are made of atoms. No one has seen even the smallest atom; you could put a million on the head of a pin. But the atom is huge compared with the particles inside it.

The particles making it up, like electrons, protons, neutrons, quarks, smaller ones still. That's what microphysics is about — the very structure, the foundation of the physical world. It's much stranger than you'd think. Mostly the atom is empty, I mean, if you think of these things as little particles in it, they don't take up much space. But the strange thing is, in a way they aren't really particles at all. They're patterns of energy, waves of energy. Or maybe only probability waves, products of equations. We don't know what, really."

"Things are made of atoms and atoms are made mostly of empty space with some energy in it? Or maybe only probabilities? It's like what I think, but you say it with science. Things...emptiness. No solidity. This bed, it's nothing. I could move through it, right through it."

She's alert now, watching me, not crying. Shakes her head. Looks like a teacher. She's going to teach me, tell me what's what.

"No, no, you don't understand. That's the miracle, the miracle of microphysics. They're so small, you can't even imagine. A particle just a billionth of what we see is called a barn because it's so big compared to the other particles. From this world of energy, this flux we cannot see or really understand, real objects emerge. Substance. Beds, tables, mountains, your own body. They are real, solid, you can't move through. But how? We don't know how. And all the small parts, or equations, we don't know yet why they work. There are such profound problems. It's chaos, bewildering beautiful chaos."

Now she looks happy. Excited, even. Weird. But it doesn't last. More tears.

"Don't cry. So if it's so wonderful and interesting, why cry?"

"I can't do it anymore. Never. Not again."

"But why?"

"You need other people, too many, too much. Results

from scientists all over the country. No, all over the world to make the smallest discovery. If you can't trust them, you don't know anything."

"So trust them. You believe tables are made of bundles of energy in space, and you don't believe people can be trusted, people you can see and talk to? That's crazy!"

"People cheat, lie, deceive. There was a fraud. All our work was for nothing, wasted because of him. A famous man, oh yes, famous, with a big reputation, a big lab. Huge grants. And he faked it, *faked* it. Everything we did was wrong because of him. Years, just wasted because we couldn't trust him. I'm not going through it again, not ever."

She can't trust anyone? If she really means it, she needs help. More than me. But a nurse is coming. We can't talk more, not right now.

"Here's breakfast. Now you make sure you get a lot to eat. You're much too skinny."

First, a shaking heap. It turns into a patient, then a professor, talks of mysteries and energy. Now it's a mother. 'Eat, you should eat.' Don't want to look like her, bruised, skinny, stringy. I'll eat.

Patient Report: Caitlin M. June 2, 1988

Greatly improved. Eating. Relates well to Ellen T. Thinking more clearly. Arguing, seems more rational, but still refuses to accept the 'substantiality' of her own body.

J. Weinstein, Psychiatrist

Patient Report: Ellen T. June 2, 1988

Somewhat improved. Relates well to Caitlin M. Over-intellectualizing. Yet no connection between confidence in CM and general paranoia, especially regarding scientists.

J. Weinstein, Psychiatrist

They say I'm better now. Mom and Dad came twice. Yesterday they said I looked pretty. Had my hair brushed out smooth, and it's still blond. My blush on, my blue nightie. And she looks better too. Quite good considering how old she is. She wore mascara, lipstick, and a pink housecoat when Mom and Dad were here. Dad brought us flowers — red and purple tulips, makes the yellow here look like sun. Outside are trees, with the early spring pale green leaves. It's just the beginning of spring, we won't miss it all being in here. In the park little kids in strollers, bigger ones running, playing on slides and climbers. Wearing shorts, some of them.

Dad said we might move out of here soon. There are earthquake warnings. Ellen didn't care. She said, 'Don't worry, they don't know what they're talking about.' She meant the scientists — still doesn't trust them. Mom and Dad looked at her a little strange. Funny, I wouldn't worry either. Rocks and all those things that might fall on you, they're really nothing. Only in the mind. Even in science, they're just space, filled with just a few teeny particles that aren't even really particles at all. Mom and Dad looked worried when Ellen and I were talking about this. But really, I think they like her all right.

I do too. She understood about the flying and she's fun to argue with. We keep talking about all kinds of things like food, diets, being young and old. And out-of-body experiences, and whether matter is solid. She keeps saying she doesn't trust anybody, but I don't think she acts that way. Not to Mom and Dad and me, anyway. Or even to Dr. Weinstein. Old winey Weinstein. She's old, but she's better than my friends. Better to talk to. They think I'm nuts when I tell them about the mountain, and how things aren't solid. Better than Mom and Dad. They won't take me seriously, won't really listen. Too busy being parents, worrying about whether I eat enough, whether I'm ever going smarten up and act normal.

We sure do have some funny talks, though. Well, there's not much else to do. We have a lot of time in here, between showers and meals and seeing Dr. Weinstein. Oh, and group therapy. But the others don't want to talk about microphysics and whether things are real, not on your life. Weinstein says, 'Well, what can you expect?' Weinstein, authority on being sane. Makes us not-crazy. Together. Or can he?

She tries to explain this microphysics. Crazy, I'll learn more in here than I ever do in school. She's really grabbed by this stuff, even though she keeps saying you can't trust science and scientists. I can't believe she's giving it up, the way she keeps saying she's going to.

She told me with this small stuff, the electrons and smaller, nothing's definite the way scientists used to think it was. They can't predict things, there aren't causes the way they used to think. Can't even completely describe the way things are. Electrons and photons, units of light she said they were, they are supposed to be both waves and particles. Somehow they are both and neither and they show up different things when the scientists do different sorts of experiments. We only know all this stuff by the effects scientists get.

How things are depends on how the scientists treat them. So, she says, somehow mind and matter have to be connected. And for her the problem isn't with matter. Not like me. It's that the scientists' minds might go wrong. Because she doesn't trust them. She says in microphysics mind and matter can't be completely separated. It's like my idea that matter is just an illusion, something your mind makes up. Only she didn't like it when I said that.

She told me about this man Heisenberg. About fifty years ago he showed you can't predict what electrons will do. You can't say where an electron will be a few minutes from now, even a few seconds from now, because it's impossible to know enough about it. You can't both put it in a place and give it a speed. Not both at once. So, she says, you can't predict where it's going to be. It's indefinite.

I tried to tell her she thinks just like me. There's nothing real there, not anything solid. If beds and stuff are made out of all these little energy packets that depend on the mind and can't be fully understood, and stuff, they might as well be nothing. They're not substantial, not material. There's nothing to objects, really. The solid bed or table, even your own body, it must be an illusion in a way. But she didn't go for that. Oh no. Even with all this weird stuff, she likes to insist on 'common sense'. That's what we argue about.

"You can't deny the real world, Caitlin. It doesn't make sense. All our language and thought comes from this, words, ordinary life. The words you use yourself — "bed", "steak", "solid". If you say you don't believe in the world, the real world, you just make yourself ridiculous. Your actions show you wrong every time. You're on a bed, under a sheet, you're wearing that blue T-shirt you call a nightie, you can talk to me about what I wear and what we eat. Of course you believe in the material world. It's mere pretense to say otherwise. Hypocrisy and nonsense."

"But that's not what science says, you told me yourself. It shows objects are mostly empty space, partly particles but not really particles, half waves, energy packets, no one knows what. In indefinite states, doing unpredictable things. That's what we know about this solid material world we're supposed to believe by common sense."

"There's no choice, Caitlin, no real option. The only question is how to fit the ordinary world and the world of microphysics together. They're both real."

She stares at me hard, straightens her glasses.

"Ellen, you're too straight, too much the professor. Loosen up, think where we are. You give me the perfect argument, perfect for the doctors, even my parents. Scientists study objects, right? The material world. And they find out what things are like, how they work. Solidity, reality — nothing. Experience is real. When I flew to the mountain, came outside my body, then I knew. Nothing. My mind went right through."

It was so wonderful, but I can't seem to get anyone to understand how things were. How things are — that other reality.

"Caitlin, be serious. I told you, if anything wasn't solid, it was your mind, not these objects. You felt you were flying and you had a fabulous experience. Nice, nice. But the world is still real. If you don't accept that it is, you're never going to get out of here."

Get out of here. Yeah. I guess I want to, though now I'm almost having fun. It's pretty crazy — ha ha — but it's true.

"Tell me this, if common sense is so sensible. How can things be so indefinite and fuzzy at this really tiny level and still be solid and predictable when they are ordinary and middle-sized? Doesn't any of this fuzziness seep through? I don't see how a reliable middle-sized world can be made up of a random and strange micro world. Doesn't all that flux of particles or whatever they are make strange things happen in the common sense world that you're so sure exists?"

"Maybe, maybe it does. Scientists are working on this.

There's a story about it actually, what they call a thought experiment. A cat, that will be killed by an electric current, but only if there is one of these quantum effects that we can't

know or predict. Schrodinger's cat — it's named after a famous physicist. They say the cat is neither dead nor alive until some scientist observes it. It's just in there, in no condition at all, because the quantum effect isn't one way or the other until there is an observer, and whether the cat is alive or dead depends on the quantum effect. That's hard to understand. Schrodinger made it up and even he could hardly believe it. But still, it doesn't deny common sense; Schrodinger still believed that cats exist, and all the quantum things do too. You're a bright girl, Caitlin. You'll go far when you get out of this place, come out of this phase."

I'm bright, very bright, but in a phase. Ellen, your age is

showing. Now you sound just like my mother. I'll go far? What does it mean? This stuff is fine, in here, and the out-of-body experience was great. Yeah, maybe I'll go far out of my body. But that's not what she means. Would I want to be a career woman? A professor like her? A mother?

"Now lots of my students don't argue as well as you, and they're older and through several years of university. They lack your intensity, yes, that's natural, but also your skills at logic. It's good. Good to really think about what things mean. But you mustn't overdo it. Science itself has to assume ordinary things are real, whatever scientists later discover when they do their complicated experiments."

That teacher look again. "Why do you say that?" Now she looks impatient. But interested, she's always interested.

"Silly, they need apparatus — cloud chambers, mirrors, magnets, accelerators, lights, and so much more. Every idea is checked by many experiments, involving many people. They don't just sit and think, or lie in bed talking and arguing like us. They do experiments, with equipment. If they started saying their own equipment was illusory, they'd sound pretty stupid."

"Let me see if I get this. They have to believe in a real solid world, to do experiments. Then they do experiments, and they get all these strange results. This microphysics, quantum stuff. All this stuff shows things are made of empty space with energy packets in it, in conditions we can never completely describe. Is that it?"

"Sort of. Well, in a way, but..."

"So if you assume the world is real and sensible and start investigating it using science, real modern science, you find out it isn't real and it isn't sensible. Right?"

She isn't going to like this one. Looks annoyed, then amused, kind of. You can imagine her being a prof, sitting in a suit behind a desk. Or in a lab, wearing those smeary glasses and a crumpled white coat.

"Caitlin, Caitlin, you've almost echoed Bertrand Russell." Laughs. "Goodness, it's a long time since anybody made me think about this sort of thing. Look, this is philosophy, not physics. We know things are real, solid, we have a common sense everyday picture of the world. And science gives us another picture, these days a very strange one, one we can't fit together, for the smallest parts of things. The job is to fit these pictures together. We have to figure out how these strange worlds of particles or waves can give us our own real solid world. It's a problem, a deep mystery, I know. But the answer can't be that the ordinary real world is only an illusion. That's the miracle, the incomprehensible thing Einstein spoke about, the problem we are trying to solve."

"Two pictures? I can't grasp the science picture at all. To me, it just doesn't make sense. And what you call common sense doesn't either. You have two pictures, maybe. I have none."

Sure, she sounds logical enough when you just listen. But none of it fits together. There's no whole, not like what I saw on the mountain.

"It's hard, I know, but it works. We use it to make things you know, like televisions and computers. It's a careful working model, not just science fiction."

"You're going back, then. I know you will. Research professor, microphysics. It's your life."

"I don't know. It was my life. I thought science was objective, didn't think about the people in it. Now I know better. You know, the quantum world — one other thing that makes it unique and hard to understand is the way people are involved in knowing objects. These states of micro-matter, quantum states they sometimes call them. They are indefinite, they become definite only when we measure them. It's people who measure, and if you can't trust them, you have nothing. If we measure different things—wave-type things or particle-type things, we have different results. You can't separate what is observed from the person observing it, that's how they put it. Not the way old-fashioned science thought you could. People, and science, and what matter is—it's all mixed up. Too much. I don't trust the others. Can't anymore, that's the problem."

Matter is measure, and measure is people, and people can't be trusted. She's not as sensible as she sounds. Oh no, we've come to that point again. Her eyes are filling up. She sniffs, wipes her glasses, pretending not to cry.

Such an empty life she seems to have. No man, no children, only these strange experiments in this microphysics. Not what I want for myself. It's fun to think and argue, but I want to love and live. The spinster professor. Kind of sad.

Patient Report: Caitlin M. June 6, 1988

Patient looks and seems well. Talks, argues brightly. Eccentric ideas persist on the reality of matter. Seems more a philosophical eccentricity than a psychological disorder.

J. Weinstein

Patient Report: Ellen T. June 6, 1988

Patient greatly improved. Appearance quite acceptable, suspicion of others greatly diminished, now directed exclusively towards scientists, whom she claims not to trust. Expresses extraordinary interest in common sense philosophies. Evidence, perhaps, of persistent tendency to over-intellectualize, not to face her own needs and emotions.

J. Weinstein

Recommended Treatments:

Both patients essentially well, but unusually committed to peculiar philosophical discussion. No further psychiatric treatment required. Philosopher recommended, through call to Dr. T. Weinstein. May be released early without risk if earthquake evacuation necessary.
(General evacuation may be required June 9.) (JW)

He's getting a philosopher. His brother—would you believe it? This Weinstein guy is a twin, and his brother is a philosopher. Just our luck. He thinks we're cured, that's the good news, but that we're philosophically confused. Ha ha. That is, we don't agree with him, and we don't agree with lots of people. But we seem sane enough, and we eat stuff, and look OK, and argue and talk a lot. So we're not crazy any more. We just have a philosophical problem. His brother is supposed to come in and solve it for us.

If there's time. They're still worried about the earthquake. He says it's good we're better, because everybody in the ward might have to be sent somewhere else. You have to admit, rocks and shakes could move us out of here, they say we might have to go. Sure, reality is solid enough for that, but it's only because of other people, what they think.

That must be him. Weinstein Two, the great philosopher.

"The problem is pictures, pictures and language. Scientists have a mathematical language, and it doesn't hook onto our ordinary words. These so called objects of microphysics — the electrons, protons, neutrons, quarks, waves, whatever — the problem is with the words we use to describe them."

Weinstein, the other Weinstein. One wasn't enough. He looks quite a bit like the Doctor. Pudgy, pocked skin, with that kind of curly hair, partly brown, partly gray. Nice brown eyes. Looks kind of cuddly — till he starts talking at you.

"The problem is words? Don't reduce it all to words. We say things aren't solid, aren't real, substantial. Because there are too many spaces, and only unpredictable flashes of electric energy. She admits it, really, even a professor. Science has discovered the real world has no matter in it. Things aren't solid and substantial at all." I wanted to make him feel it.

"Caitlin, please. You make me sound so adolescent. I didn't go *that* far."

"Maybe not quite. I know you wanted to hang onto common sense. But you couldn't answer me. I'm just saying, though, I'm trying to tell him, it's *not* only words. It's serious."

"Look, I'll try to explain what I mean. When we talk, we use words from life, and that's the only way we can talk. Or think, for that matter. Life is on a middle-sized level, mostly. Our words are adjusted to everyday, to our experience of tables and floors and flowers and foods. Microphysics is billions of times smaller in scale, you see, and the words just don't fit. We try to make them fit but the more we try the more confused we are. When you say an electron is both a wave and a particle, then it's wrong, all wrong, because both these words are from the ordinary middle-sized world. Same with "real" and "solid". They just won't fit, and we only get ourselves confused when we try to make them fit."

"How do you mean? I don't really get it."

"These words only mean something when we use them in a situation we can relate to ordinary life, where we know what they mean. Take the word "solid." Just think about it. Think of something that's solid. A good firm table or a plank of wood. It will support you if you stand on it, you can't put your hand through it. It doesn't have holes, no pores, it's not a gas or a liquid. OK it's solid. We give a meaning to a word like "solid" when we use it, and we use it for things like these. It doesn't make sense to say these things, things like tables aren't solid, because then you try to use "solid" with some new meaning it never had. Things we all call solid *are* solid. Try to use words differently from everybody else, and nobody will understand what you're saying. In fact, you don't even really understand it yourself."

"Come on, it's not that simple. That's philosophy? It's just boring, nothing new."

"Who said everything true has to be exciting? Things may sound dull to you, but that doesn't mean they're not true. That's how it is, it's how language works. And you can get yourselves into some humdinger problems by forgetting it. "Real," "substantial," even "matter," "material," they're all the same in this way. Science can't show ordinary life and ordinary language are wrong, because scientists are just like everybody else. They only make sense when they use words in normal ordinary ways that other people can understand."

"But science has a whole new picture of reality. She told me."

"Caitlin, please. Don't use me too much. Science doesn't say things are mostly empty space, that nothing's solid or substantial! I didn't tell you your mind could go through a mountain and science doesn't either. None of that. Those are your ideas. Not mine, not from science. Ther' are two different pictures of the world, from common sense and from science, and the job is to fit them together. We haven't fit them together yet, but when we do we'll understand how things work."

"Look, that's better, but not quite it. It's hard, I know, but even this is wrong. The thing is, there aren't two pictures."

This guy is irritating. I want to push him on these arguments. I mean, he's so nice in a way, but it's maddening, he's such a smooth talker and he's so damned sure of himself. Cool. For him the world's so cool, all so organized, no mysteries. He's trying to help, but he bugs me. *"What's* so hard?"

Cool. For him, the world's so cool.

"Accepting that there's no scientific picture of the world. Not in microphysics anyway. The level is too small, too remote from experience. There are just equations, predictions, calculations, experiments. But we can't use all this to get a picture. Not of the little pellets of matter the scientists used to think about a century ago, and not of the tiny particles and subparticles and waves and energy packets people talk about now. Sure, we say matter is energy, but even that's not quite right at this level. Because our mind wants to picture using words we know, which are all we have, and the level is just too small. By orders of magnitude. You and Ellen understand that science, in microphysics, doesn't give us a common sense picture of objects. But what you haven't understood is that it gives us *no picture* whatsoever. You try to make another picture, with empty space, force fields, waves, or unpredictable particles, or whatever. And that's where you're going wrong. There is no picture for it. None at all. We have to understand without a picture, without our ordinary words and images, and that's what makes it so hard."

I'm looking at Ellen. Can't she say anything? He's trying to dissolve our mysteries, and it makes me kind of sad.

"I read some Zen once, you know, when I was taking a break from teaching."

Good, she's going to answer him. I'm not up to it, quite. I mean, a philosopher! They argue all the time. It's way worse than talking to a physics professor.

"Zen? And what did you think of it? Never made much sense to me."

"Nor to me. But there was something in it, something that reminds me of what you're telling us now. About questions. Some questions can't be answered. The answer is only that there is no question. That's the only thing you can come to understand."

"OK, OK. Yeah, that's just about it. I never would have thought Zen would help, but that's just right. If the question is, 'how do we picture things at the micro level, the basic fundamental structure of matter?', the answer is, 'we don't picture them'. We can't. But it's hard to accept it."

"It is indeed." She looks partly satisfied, but maybe not quite. "For the micro level we have equations and we have words we can't really understand, because we use them for a world too small, too small to handle with our concepts. We can't fit a picture with common sense, can't link it up, because there's no picture at all. God, I see what you're saying, but it's hard to take. I want more — real fit. Real understanding."

She still looks a little doubtful.

Two professors, and they only want to turn the problem off. Never solve it. Can't you do better than this?

They evacuated the next day. And there was a quake too, not as serious as the scientists predicted, I guess, but still bad enough to crack the building and break a few windows. Including the one in the lounge, right next to our old room.

We could have been hurt, so I guess you have to say they were right to move us. But I miss the place a bit.

We still see Ellen, because she bought the condo next to ours. It's good for her to have the company, and I'm always happy when she comes for weekends. She brings students sometimes. Scruffy types — no cute guys. But they're fun to talk to, and they'll talk about weird things if you want. Just like her, I guess. She's teaching again, but she isn't doing any research, says she's too tired. I think it's not wanting to work with the others. She'll swallow all the stuff from common sense, she listens to the Weinsteins and to Mom and Dad and me too. But she can't believe in other scientists enough to work with them, so she still doesn't want to get into research. Or so she says. She was hurt too much by that fraud. No trust, no science. Even the Weinsteins couldn't handle that problem.

Am I better? Sure — my problems are only philosophical now. I'm not crazy, I just get funny ideas sometimes, or so they say. I'm OK. I didn't have any more out-of-body experiences. Not yet, but I'd sure like to some day. With the Weinsteins, or better still, the whole family. Dreamer, dreamer. We could all go off together on an out-of-body trip. (Just kidding, just kidding.)

CONSCIENCE

Chris: Hi, Robin. I haven't seen you for a while.

Robin: No, I've been off seeing my grandmother. She wanted me to visit and I kept putting it off. Finally my conscience was really bothering me, so I decided to cancel some other things and go.

Jan: You thought it was your duty?

Robin: Yeah, I guess so. She's hard to talk to, but she's so lonely and she really needs more people around. My parents and my brother and I are the only family she's got, and we owe her that much.

Chris: Your conscience told you to go, so you went? Boy, are you superstitious!

Robin: What do you mean, superstitious?

Chris: Believing in a little voice in your head that knows what you should do and doing what it tells you? I don't know.

Robin: Is that what you think conscience is? A little voice in the head?

Chris: I don't think conscience is particularly anything. I'm not sure it even exists. But it seems to me other people think it's a voice in the head.

Jan: It's just a way of talking, Chris, for heaven's sake. Your conscience is that part of you that knows what you should do and what you shouldn't do, and reminds you about it. It makes you feels guilty when you do something you know is wrong. You know, morality. Everybody has a conscience.

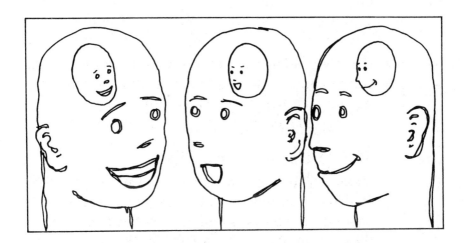

Chris: If everybody has a conscience why would George Bush need an ethics advisor? Shouldn't his own conscience tell him what's right and wrong?

Jan: I guess he's too busy to pay attention to it or something. But let's stay away from politics, Chris. Stick to the topic.

Robin: Isn't God supposed to give you your conscience, to help you do the right thing?

Chris: So God would be the one who reminded you to go and see your grandmother?

Robin: Don't be silly, I didn't say *that*. No, I mean when you and Jan say these things, it starts me thinking about what conscience is. I never really thought about it before. I always think of myself as having a conscience that can remind me what to do, but maybe I shouldn't think that way, since I'm not really very religious. Do you have to believe in God to believe in a conscience?

Jan: Oh I don't think so, Robin. Your conscience is supposed to give you knowledge of morality, not religion. But the conscience isn't a little thing in the brain, or a little voice in the head, not exactly.

Chris: We've got something in us that tells us what's right and wrong, but it's not a little thing in the brain? This sounds like unscientific nonsense!

Robin: My conscience is just whatever it is in me that knows what I ought to do. When I say my conscience is bothering me, I just mean I've done something I shouldn't have done — or I haven't done something I should have done. And I'm feeling guilty. It's my conscience that makes me feel guilty for things I do and don't do.

Jan: That's how I think about it. Your conscience is for morality, for things about moral principles and duties to other people and so on. Ethics. Not just practical things like whether you take up jogging or tidy up your room or get organized for the next exam. And not religion — who created the earth and heaven and hell, and the devil and so on.

Chris: I don't know. You can say conscience is that part of you that knows what is morally right and morally wrong. Sure, nice definition. But how *do* you know what's morally right and morally wrong? That's the problem. Maybe nobody does.

Robin: I guess that's why I thought conscience might have

something to do with religion. You know, the Ten Commandments and so on. That's what a lot of people think morality is. And it is supposed to have come as the word of God, when God gave the Ten Commandments to Moses.

Chris: Well, the Ten Commandments will only take you so far. They certainly don't solve all the moral problems people get into today. It's been a long time since Moses.

Jan: I don't think anybody thinks the Ten Commandments will tell you what to do if a mugger tries to take your mother's wallet and you're wondering whether to try to fight back.

Chris: Or whether there should be test-tube babies.

Jan: Or what a hospital should do if there are ten patients who need a kidney transplant and there is only one available kidney.

Chris: It's not so easy, is it? People disagree all the time about what should be done. We can say we have a conscience to tell us what is right and wrong. But what *is* right and wrong, and how do you know it? Religion doesn't help too much, as far as I can tell.

Robin: Wouldn't it help? I mean, if you were religious, then you would go to a church and they would tell you what God thinks people should do.

Chris: But there isn't just one religion. There are lots and lots, and they say different things about what people should do. According to some religions, men can have four wives; according to others, only one. According to some, cows are sacred animals, according to others, people shouldn't eat pigs.

According to others, they should eat no meat at all, according to others it doesn't matter. Even if there is a God who is telling us what we should do, it is sure hard to understand what He is saying!

Robin: I don't know, Chris. Many people sure think morality comes from religion. They have faith, they believe in God, go to church, and are told in Sunday school and in sermons what they should and shouldn't do. That's where their morality comes from. You know the saying: If God is dead, all is permitted. That just says morality depends on believing in God, and if we don't believe in Him, there's no distinction between right and wrong. Is all this stuff just wrong?

Chris: Yep. I don't know what conscience is and I don't know whether there's any such thing as a correct or true morality, but I do know you can't get a reliable morality out of religion. There are too many different religions. They're mostly based on different books written too long ago, and they say different things. Lots of them are pretty irrational, as far as I can make out.

Jan: Such confidence! Actually, I agree with you though. Morality *doesn't* depend on religion.

Robin: You two are so sure of yourselves! It must be nice. I don't think it's all that easy, Chris.

Jan: Usually I'm on your side in these arguments, Robin, but today I'm with Chris. I don't think it really makes sense to think of morality coming from religion. Look, suppose there were no standard of goodness at all, apart from what God said.

Robin: OK, let's suppose. Then what?

Jan: Well, then God could approve of anything whatever, right? He wouldn't have to conform to any moral standards, because there wouldn't be any, apart from what He said and did.

Robin: Right. He would be the only source for what was right and wrong. That makes sense, Jan. God is God. If He exists, He's supreme. You remember — the Greatest Conceivable Being. He doesn't depend on anything else, and He sure isn't going to be bowing down to moral standards or any other kind of standards that come from anywhere else.

Jan: Well, God could approve of torturing small babies, if He didn't have to conform to any moral standards. Right? I mean, we think torture like this would be wrong, but that doesn't mean God would have to conform.

Chris: Good grief, Jan. I'm not religious or anything, but isn't that a bit much? Surely God would never approve of anything like that!

Jan: That's not the point, Chris. If you're so sure that God wouldn't approve of torturing babies, then that just shows you're think of God as a morally virtuous being. The Greatest Conceivable in virtue as well as everything else. No god would ever approve of something like torturing small babies. The reason is that torturing small babies is something that would be awfully, horribly, wrong. God, or a god, in any religion, is a being we are supposed to worship, and He's worshipped partly because of Goodness. God is supposed to be good, so God couldn't approve of torturing innocent creatures.

Robin: Well all right, Jan, so why are you trying to get us to imagine it? It doesn't make sense.

Jan: The point is, Robin, torture is just plain wrong and we know it. We know it's wrong, quite apart from anything we know about God or any god, and it's just because we know this that it would be so absurd to think God could ever approve of such a thing.

Chris: For religious believers, God is Good. He is supremely good.

Jan: Right. And that makes sense. It makes sense because we have a standard of goodness, we have some idea of what goodness is, and we need this, when we think of divine beings as being good.

Robin: I don't know, Jan. You make it sound so clear-cut. Is it really all that simple?

Chris: Are you saying that if God is good, then the standard of what's good must be something independent of God? Something God didn't just invent or make up?

Jan: That's it. If it weren't, then saying God is good would only mean that He lives up to His own standards, and that wouldn't be any achievement. I mean, even the Devil lives up to his own standards.

Robin: If there is one, and if he has standards...

Chris: If you're right, then moral judgments can't depend on religion. We need some idea of good to have a religion in the first place.

Jan: That's just it. There's got to be some other notion of morality, and that's what is appealed to when God is seen as good.

Robin: OK, so if we go along with this, then, getting back to conscience, conscience doesn't have to be dependent on teachings from religion. Our conscience is that part of us that knows what's right and what's wrong. Morality comes from our own conscience, from ourselves, from that part of ourselves that can distinguish right from wrong. Our conscience is something in us, some sense of ethics that we have on our own.

Chris: Robin, you're just talking around in circles. You say conscience is the part of us that knows what's right and wrong. But how would we know what's right and wrong? Not from the preachers, not from the Bible or other religious books, not even straight from God. Just from our conscience. Our conscience tells us what's right and wrong, and we know what's right and wrong because our conscience tells us? This isn't going anywhere... Maybe there is just nothing to know about right and wrong. Maybe there are no correct answers, and conscience is just a myth.

Robin: How could conscience be a myth? My conscience told me to go to see my grandmother. You know your conscience would bother you if you stole something or cheated on an exam, or lied to a friend. You'd feel guilty, and that's one reason you wouldn't do it in the first place. Conscience is absolutely real, and we experience it every day of our lives.

Chris: If you define conscience as that part of us that knows the difference between right and wrong, it's a myth. Because no part of us knows the difference between right and wrong. We can't prove anything about it, and we just don't know.

Jan: Don't we know some things we can't exactly prove? By experience, or intuition, or something?

Chris: Maybe in some cases; I'm not sure. But you can't say this for morality. There's just too much disagreement. People have too many different ideas on what is right and wrong. Think of abortion, for instance. Some people are just positive it's a terrible sin or crime, just the same as murder. But others think it's quite acceptable, and something women should be able to do to have control over their lives. That disagreement exists right within our own society. If you consider what people believe about morality the world over, just about anything goes.

Robin: Like Saudi Arabia, where women aren't allowed to drive or hold jobs?

Chris: Well, that's a legal thing, but I guess the law is based on their moral code. They believe women should be separate from men and work and live in their own space. So who's right, us or them? We think their customs for men and women deny women's rights, and they think ours lead to terrible things like sexual disease and divorce and pornography. How can we say who's got the answer? We only know what we think is right. And they think it's wrong.

Jan: That's not even the most extreme example you could take either. There are societies where infants are killed right after birth, and that's con-

134

sidered quite acceptable. Especially if they're girls. And where old people are left alone to die in the cold. One of the most awful, I think, is what they used to do in India with widows. If a man died, his wife would be buried alive with him, and they were burned in a funeral ceremony. This meant if your husband died before you, you were likely to be burned alive. The idea was that the wife was supposed to keep her husband company in the life after death. It was called suttee.

Robin: But it doesn't happen any more, does it? I mean, people in India came to understand that it was wrong.

Jan: Let's hope it's gone forever. People must know it's wrong.

Chris: They *believe* it's wrong, you mean.

Robin: Come on Chris, you don't really mean what you're saying. You can't mean that burning someone alive is something we don't know is wrong. The suffering would be just incredible!

Jan: Chris, are you saying that because different societies have different ideas about what's right and wrong, nobody knows what's right and wrong? I don't think that would be a very convincing argument. People disagree about other things, and just because they disagree we don't conclude that nobody knows what's true, that there's no knowledge. Different opinions and beliefs can have lots of explanations.

Robin: We can't say that just because there is disagreement between societies, no one at all knows what's

135

right and wrong.

Jan: Maybe some of the differing societies are incorrect. Maybe the disagreements will go away when people understand the real facts, or when they have a chance to communicate with each other. If different groups disagree, there can still be truth. It might be something different from both their ideas — or one group might turn out to be right in the end.

Chris: OK, Jan, that's possible but it isn't the point. The point is we don't have any way of knowing who has the right answer. Each society is convinced its own way is right and the others are wrong. Who are we to say? You hear about women being kept behind the veil, or about suttee, or killing infants, and you feel horrified and furious. You may feel sure our practices are right and these are wrong. But that doesn't prove anything. People in other societies probably feel just as sick and horrified thinking about things that go on here — like old parents being left in institutions, instead of with their sons and daughters. And divorce, and so on.

Robin: So what are you saying, Chris? That what's right and what's wrong depend completely on what society you're in? What a society thinks is right just *is* right, for them? Like in Saudi Arabia, it really would be morally wrong for a woman to drive a car, and in New Guinea, where people used to eat their enemies, cannibalism was quite all right?

Chris: That's it. Sure, I know it sounds strange when you say it just like that. But that's because we're so much within our own society. We may think we

understand other societies but we really don't.
We can't judge what they are doing. You can only
understand a culture and make a judgment about
it, from inside.

Robin: First I thought you were saying that we do know
when other people are doing the right thing.
They're acting in the right way when they follow
their own societies' teachings. But then you seem
to turn around and say we don't know, because we
can't get far enough inside another culture or
society to make a judgment about it. I don't get it.
Be consistent! *Do* people know what's right and
wrong for them to do? Or don't they?

Jan: You said we can't say whether they're doing what's
right or wrong, if we really don't understand the
culture. But then, if it's right to do whatever the
culture says, and that's what they're doing, they
must be right. You're confused!

Chris: What I mean is, all people can do is act according
to the moral teachings of whatever society they're
in. We have to do this with our society and other
people have to do it with theirs. Nobody knows
what to do, I guess. I mean, you couldn't say we
know it's right for Saudi Arabian women to follow
the teachings in Saudi Arabia. But we can't make
judgments or interfere, that's what I'm trying to
say.

Jan: So what do you think conscience is, then? You
still want to say it's a myth?

Chris: Conscience comes from the way we're brought up.
It only reminds us of what we've been taught is
right and wrong, and makes us feel guilty when we

do things we know we shouldn't. That just comes from what we're taught. My mother taught me not to take candy out of the store unless we paid for it, and that's why I'd feel guilty if I stole something. My conscience would bother me — meaning, the way I was brought up would make me think I shouldn't do it. If they'd brought me up another way, I'd feel differently.

Jan: If you'd been brought up to be a pickpocket or a drug dealer, you'd have a different conscience?

Chris: Absolutely. I'd feel guilty if I ratted on my buddies to the police.

Robin: And if you'd been brought up as a Nazi, you'd feel guilty if you didn't turn Jews in to the police?

Chris: Right.

Robin: I don't think you really believe that. I just don't. Everyone knows things like the Golden Rule — Don't do unto others what you would not have them do unto you. Nazis knew that. They knew they were doing things that were wrong. They knew Jews were people who loved their children, and wanted to live, and suffered from starvation and pain and cold and brutality. They did things to the Jews they would never have accepted for themselves, and it wasn't because they didn't know it was wrong. Not because they didn't have a conscience. They had a conscience all right. But they just didn't listen to it. They hid what they were doing from themselves, lied to themselves, tried to justify themselves. To think that Nazis were following their conscience! It's just one more lie for us to think any of them were really sincere in doing what they thought was right.

Jan: To me this whole business about morality being relative to what the society or group believes is just one giant cop-out. It's an excuse for not facing up to the real problems.

Robin: How do you mean?

Jan: It's the lazy person's morality. If somebody has a moral problem, he is supposed to think to himself, 'Now let me see, what does my social group teach about this? Would it be right to do such-and-such? What do other people say?' It's as if the only way you can think about what you should do is to ask what other people think they should do, and what they think you should do. Nobody's supposed to think as an individual, but somehow groups are supposed to know what to do. It doesn't make sense. From what you say, morality is no more than some kind of herd instinct. Everybody tries to follow the others, and nobody really thinks at all.

Chris: Where have you been, Jan? Isn't that just the way people *do* react to moral problems? They are always worried about what other people will think about what they do.

Robin: Suppose somebody was pregnant and she didn't want to be. She might try to decide whether to have an abortion. She would start really thinking about whether this could ever be a right thing for anyone to do, and about whether it would be the right thing for her to do, and so on. It would be a terrible problem. But I don't think she'd try to solve it just by trying to find out what teachings her social group had. If she did hear those teachings, wouldn't she wonder whether they were correct or not? Anyway, we don't have agreement about abortion in our society. There isn't any one teaching to appeal to. When you pick the people you're asking, you're deciding what to think. Ask a priest, you'll get one answer. Ask a feminist, you'll get another.

Chris: There is just no answer to a problem like that.

Jan: Great! Boy, if anybody has a big moral problem, let's hope they don't come to you for advice!

Chris: Don't blame it all on me, Jan. I didn't make up this mess. How can anybody really give advice in a situation like that? You can only do what you've been taught, and if you haven't been taught anything, because the society doesn't have a clear teaching, then there is just no answer.

Robin: So what do you *do*, for heaven's sake, if you get into one of these problems? People have got to be able to figure out for themselves what they should do. We have to have our own beliefs and know our own feelings. Everybody has sympathy for others and a natural conscience for things like the Golden Rule.

Jan: I just thought of another problem. Not only do some societies, like ours, disagree about things like abortion, but there are lots of people who are actually members of several different societies at the same time. You couldn't just tell them to follow what the group says, because they are in several groups that say quite different things.

Robin: What do you mean?

Chris: Yeah, I'm not quite sure I get the point. Sure, lots of people are members of several groups, but so what?

Jan: Well, think of families from places like Iran and India, who live in North America, or families from Turkey, say, who live in western European countries like Holland. They are caught between two different societies — in both, or in neither, you might say. If you follow Chris's idea that a person should do whatever his social group has taught him to do, this sure won't help, because the two societies tell them different things.

Chris: They're in two social groups and the groups have different moral rules?

Jan: Right. One may say it's a moral obligation to get a job for your relative or to bribe an official, whereas the other says you have to advertise jobs openly and consider all applicants fairly, and officials shouldn't be bribed. One may say women shouldn't bare their legs, while the other permits bikinis or even topless swimming and sunbathing. People who live in these situations do have to make decisions. They can't just look for a social code and think, 'oh yes, that's what everybody else does, so that's what we'll do too.'

Robin: There might not even be anybody else in just the same situation.

Jan: Even if there were, who is to say that what that other person decided to do is the right thing?

Robin: That's the problem. I mean, even in the situation where there is just one social group and it does have an answer, based on a social rule, it's still possible the group might give you the wrong answer. You shouldn't just follow the herd when you have an important decision to make.

Chris: I don't know about you two. What's the standard you use, when you say these groups might be *wrong*? Who are you to say? Who is anybody to say? I think this kind of idea that there is a right answer, or a right solution to a moral problem is just plain dangerous. And there's no foundation for it, really. You just believe in it because you want to.

Robin: We want to believe in it, and it makes sense too. But what's so dangerous about this idea? We have a conscience and sometimes we can know, ourselves, what's right and wrong. I don't see anything dangerous about this. It's much more dangerous to think there's no limit to what's right and wrong. No limit at all. No conscience.

Jan: Chris, what makes it dangerous, to think we sometimes know what's right?

Chris: It's so intolerant, that's the thing. If you know
you're right, then you must know the others who
disagree with you are wrong. And if you're so sure
about this, how are you going to act towards them?
Are you going to try to reform them — send in
missionaries? Or armies, to make them do what
you think is right? That's the way people used to
think, when western countries had colonies in Asia
and Africa. Now we understand it was all a big
mistake. Different cultures work different ways,
and different people have different ideas. We
shouldn't look down on people if they don't share
our ideas, and we shouldn't try to change other
people's systems to make them like ours. That's
the kind of thing you get into if you think you know
what's right and other people don't.

Robin: So you think we should let other cultures and
groups determine for themselves what to do, and
we shouldn't interfere?

Chris: Right. And that applies to individuals too. We
shouldn't interfere with other people. Even if we
disagree and think they are doing the wrong thing.

Jan: Not ever? No matter what they're doing? Gee,
Chris, I don't know.

Robin: Look, Chris, you *do* have a conscience, and your
conscience is telling you something. It's telling
you to be tolerant towards other people, not to
interfere with them, to respect their independence
and freedom, to respect their cultures and practices, not to look down on them. Your conscience

is no illusion. It's right in you and it's recommending tolerance of others.

Robin: Jan's right, Chris. You are saying you know at least one moral obligation: you know you shouldn't interfere with others.

Chris: OK, I guess that's right. That is one thing I've learned about morality: to be tolerant.

Jan: This principle of tolerance, you say it's something you've learned. But I don't know whether you mean you worked this principle out, or that it's something our society has taught you.

Chris: Well, our society has taught me this, obviously — my parents, school, even politics. I learned it when I was young, and I guess I didn't really think about it. But now I can think about it, I can reflect and judge, and when I do, I still think it's right. We should be tolerant of what other people believe and not interfere when they're doing what they think is right.

Robin: Would tolerance be wrong for a group that didn't believe in it?

Chris: I don't know quite what you mean.

Jan: There are lots of groups that think tolerance is a complete mistake. Think of the Islamic fundamentalists, with their ideas of holy war and so on. Or Christian fundamentalists, for that matter, who think people who don't share their religion are going to go to hell. They would say if you're tolerant of different religious beliefs, you are ignoring your religious duty, and ignoring an opportunity to save other people from an eternity of

144

anguish in hell.

Robin: For these people, the idea of tolerating other systems is just as awful as the idea of torturing babies is for us.

Chris: Well, that's wrong, for sure. Every group has to recognize they could be wrong, and they shouldn't try to pressure others into sharing their ideas.

Robin: 'Has to?' 'Shouldn't?' Chris, you're appealing to moral ideas they don't share. Tolerance is your moral ideal. Great, I don't disagree with you. But the point is lots of other people do disagree with you. They see tolerance as weak, or wrong, or even extremely evil.

Chris: Robin, how did we get back onto religion? Aren't we talking about religious tolerance, now? Not morality, not really.

Robin: It's all connected, Chris, because the way these people see it, morality does come straight from religion. Someone insults your religion by publishing the wrong kind of book, say. According to your religion, people who commit blasphemy are supposed to be put to death, and insulting your religion is blasphemy. So you just order his assassination. I'm not just making this up, obviously. I'm thinking about Salman Rushdie, who wrote that book *The Satanic Verses*. The Ayatollah Khomeini decided it was an insult to the Moslem religion and ordered devout Moslems to try to kill him. There was a six million dollar prize for success, and Rushdie had to go into hiding and get protection from the British police. We might not think a writer should be put to death for insulting a religion, but that's the way they look at it.

Jan: We decided that morality and religion are independent from a logical point of view, but that doesn't mean they're independent in people's minds.

Robin: They sure aren't. And wherever people get their moral convictions from, not all those convictions include tolerance. That's why what Chris says won't work. He's saying groups should do what they think, provided they all tolerate others, but then what about the groups where part of their morality is precisely that differences and criticisms shouldn't be tolerated? Whether it comes from religion or whatever, part of some moralities is intolerance.

Jan: Actually, we don't have to go to Moslem cultures to find examples of extreme disagreements about ethics which have a basis in religion. We can find the same thing right in our own society. People who are completely against abortion, and think it's murder, for instance. If you tell them they should tolerate others who believe different things, they're just furious. They think you're telling them to just stand by and let murders happen.

Jan: At least they don't order assassinations for people who argue against them!

Robin: Well not usually, anyway.

Chris: So the problem is whether we're going to tolerate people who insist that others shouldn't be tolerated? Whether we're going to tolerate intolerance?

Robin: That's it, all right.

Jan: I think we've really got you on this one, Chris. Your ideas just don't fit together. You want to say conscience is only social teaching, but you also want to say acting tolerantly to others is a moral obligation, something our conscience tells us to do. You say a society that taught intolerance, holy war, advocated missionary efforts to convert others, that sort of thing, would be wrong to do that. It would be immoral not to respect these other groups and the individuals in them. Right? Then you can't just tolerate that, because it's against your own principle of tolerance. You're not tolerating just *every* set of moral teachings. Not all equally. You have to discriminate between them.

Robin: If Jan's right, morality *isn't* just a matter of whatever a social group teaches is right. You're saying we ought to be tolerant—whether or not our society has taught us to. If somebody follows the Ayatollah and murders Rushdie because he thinks Rushdie insulted the Moslem religion, then that person will be acting intolerantly—*very* intolerantly—and he'll be doing wrong. Whether his social group and his so-called spiritual leader approves of it or not.

Chris: OK, you've got me. Morality isn't *just* a matter of following rules from your social group. Actually, maybe tolerance is a kind of higher idea, about how the different groups and different moral codes should fit together. It's a non-interference idea, sort of. I mean, each society or group could stick to its own practices and rules, and then adopt the policy of not interfering with other societies. That would avoid a lot of wars and so on, I think. People should accept each other's differences, and not think there is one answer to all the problems of life, one answer that we all have to agree on.

Robin: Would it be the same between individuals? I mean, if you believed you should do something, and I sincerely thought you were wrong, then my duty would be not to interfere unless I thought what you were going to do would hurt me? We could all go our own separate ways unless we were going to hurt each other?

Chris: I guess that's what I'm saying.

Jan: That sounds nice in theory, Chris, but I don't think it will work. People aren't separate little atoms. They all affect each other too much. Even when you are talking about different societies, still we all live on the same planet. What one individual does always affects others, sometimes for better, sometimes for worse, and what each society or social group does affects others too. The groups aren't completely distinct.

Robin: Different groups in a society are mixed together. Part of what made the Ayatollah's assassination order so frightening is that there are fundamentalist Moslems, who might follow his advice, just about all over the world. It isn't just a matter of him doing something in Iran that doesn't affect other countries. And lots of people find themselves members of several groups at once. Sure, tolerance is better than outright war. But it only takes you so far.

Chris: I don't see what you mean.

Jan: Well, think about it. Isn't it obvious? Suppose you have two societies, each in its own little country, but the countries happen to be side by side. One group says that free choice is the greatest value and that having a free economy without a lot of bureaucracy will give its people the best and happiest lives. So it has a terrific economy with lots of factories that pollute the air.

Chris: OK, Jan, but that's their choice isn't it? I mean, you might not like polluted air, but maybe they don't mind it.

Jan: Fine, Chris, fine. The only trouble is, air doesn't sit still and stay inside your country. It moves. The neighbor country might make the health of its people a very important value, and they might be pretty mad to have a lot of sick people with lung diseases that were a drain on the medicare program, and so on.

Chris: I can see what you're saying, Jan. Of course there are lots of ways countries affect each other and they have to work out compromises. But isn't tolerance at least a beginning?

Robin: Can't you just say that countries, and individuals too, shouldn't try to interfere in each others' actions unless they are being hurt themselves?

Chris: That makes sense to me.

Jan: Well, it's better than what you were saying before. But I think it's still too simple. Think of the Jews in Europe during the second world war. What the Nazis did to them didn't hurt people in Canada and the United States. And yet many people thought we should have gone in to protect them. Eventually we did enter the war, even though it wasn't only for that reason. People have some responsibility for what happens to others. If you see your neighbor brutally beating up his child, you don't just think it's a matter of his having a different lifestyle. You do something to try to protect the child.

Chris: That's just what the Islamic fundamentalists think. They know the truth, they know how people should live, and they are responsible for other human beings, for getting them to understand it too.

Jan: Chris, that's just not fair. I'm trying to say that people have limits on their behaviour, and we can't accept serious harm to ourselves or to others. Like health-destroying pollution, or governments killing and torturing minorities. There are so many really serious moral problems around. We can't appeal to different social or national or religious groups to solve them. There are too many groups, teaching too many different things, and there are too many ways all these groups depend on each other and affect each other. We don't live in a simple society where we all get taught the same thing. You just have to make up your own mind about what is right and wrong. You can't let other people do it for you.

Robin: So right and wrong depend on the individual, not the group? Whatever each person thinks is right or wrong *is* right or wrong, for him or her?

Chris: That can't be right. It would be anarchy, complete

utter confusion.

Jan: That's right, Chris. But I don't think it proves you should decide what to do by following the group. It shows when you do decide what to do, you have to seriously and honestly consider how it will affect other people. Of course you should know if other people think it's right or wrong, and why they do, but you don't always just have to go along with that.

Chris: All this thinking, though, Jan, you can't guarantee it will give you the right answer to these problems. You're telling me nothing at all really. Oh sure, you tell me what *not* to do to resolve a moral problem. You say, *don't* think you can get the answer from God or a religion. *Don't* just ask other people. *Don't* just follow a group. You're giving me terrific advice about what *not* to do. But what *do* I do? You give me one answer: I think for myself. Yeah, I follow my conscience. Sure, sure. Big deal. But *what* do I think? What does my conscience tell me? You haven't told me one single useful thing, not one.

Robin: That's not quite fair Chris. We did at least say we believed in the Golden Rule. And Jan said you have to think about how what you're doing will affect other people.

Jan: And you yourself, for that matter.

Chris: Yeah, but that's not all of morality. You can't solve your problems just with that, any more than you can figure out what to do about complicated things like test tube babies, or competition for kidney transplants, or international censorship by

151

looking it up in the Ten Commandments.

Jan: I have to grant you that. The Golden Rule says you should do unto others what you would have them do unto you. But you have to apply it just right, because not everybody likes what you like. I mean, if you like cheesecake, the Golden Rule doesn't mean you should go around giving it to everybody else. Some people don't like it.

Robin: Or they're on diets, or whatever. But I thought the Golden Rule was stated in the negative, you know, like, don't do unto others what you would not have them do unto you.

Jan: You can state it two ways, and they're different, but even with the negative way there can still be problems. Suppose you don't like people to help you with the dishes, because they get in your way in your small kitchen. So does that mean you shouldn't help anybody else, because you don't want help yourself? It would be pretty weird to think you could get an obligation not to help with the dishes out of the Golden Rule!

Chris: Great. Just great. I say you haven't told me *how* and *what* to think for myself about moral problems. Then you say, sure, we tell you to follow the Golden Rule. But then you say there are two different Golden Rules—one positive and one negative—and anyway, you have to be careful about applying them. Actually, you admit they just don't apply in some ridiculously simple situations, about whether to give out cheesecake or help with the dishes. Get serious! If I have some terrible moral problem about divorce or abortion or fighting back against a mugger, or whatever, you still haven't given me anything to go on at all. Not one thing, except you tell me what *not* to do. I had an idea, that I should do what I was taught to do, that was the basis of my conscience. Then you proved to me that wasn't right. So what do you tell me? Negative advice: I shouldn't just follow the crowd and I shouldn't misapply the Golden Rule. Big lot of help this is!

Robin: I have to admit it's not a lot to go on. No wonder people think ethical values depend on God.

Jan: But that doesn't work either. We went through it already. Look, I can't tell you a complete moral system, and tell you how to think through every problem that's going to come up. But I still think the Golden Rule — well, both Golden Rules, to be exact — have something to offer. Two things, really. First, they are telling you to think about others, not just yourself. We all care what happens to us, and lots of times we care about others, but there are always temptations to put ourselves first. The Golden Rules say others matter too.

Robin: They matter just as much as we do. A hurt is just as bad when it's yours as it is when it's mine. But we have to think sometimes, to really understand that. Usually we only feel what happens to us.

Chris: Usually. I could be psychic and feel your pain.

Robin: Come on, Chris, I thought this was a serious discussion.

Chris: So, to get back to the Golden Rule, you say it's telling us that other people are just as important as we are, when it comes to moral decisions. But there are two things, you said. What more?

Jan: Well, it's saying you have to consider what's going to happen to those other people. You have to consider the consequences of your actions for them as well as for you. Whether it would be good for them or not. It's not just whether they want cheesecake or help with the dishes, or trivial stuff like that. It's more fundamental, like whether they are really hurt, or really helped, or whether their rights are violated, whether they're respected.

Robin: If the Nazis had seriously thought of the Jews in those ways — in any one of those ways — and had really followed the Golden Rule, they just couldn't have done what they did.

Chris: Boy, are you an optimist!

Jan: I don't think so. Robin's not optimistic to say that *if* they had really considered the Jews as people equal to themselves and had cared about what happened to them, they wouldn't have beaten them and starved them and gassed them or worked them to death. That's completely obvious. What's optimistic is the first part. People don't usually think hard about what to do, and they don't consider others as important as themselves. They don't think hard enough, and they don't care enough. If they did, their conscience would have a better chance to give them proper guidance.

Robin: Maybe not all the answers, but at least enough to avoid some of these really terrible things.

Chris: Isn't there more you can say than *this*?

Jan: Well I'm not going to give you my whole theory of the universe in three minutes or less. I'm just saying there are better and worse answers, and if people really try to care about others, and think, they can figure out what to do. At least, they can do not badly. You might think this is saying nothing, but it would have been enough to avoid a lot of really awful things people have done. We just have to try to figure out what we should do, to think for ourselves, and to work out the answers. And when we do it, we have to consider other people too, not just ourselves.

Chris: And that's what your conscience tells you?

Jan: Right. That's what your conscience tells you too. Just listen.

A
Sequence
Of
Events

THE FABLE OF THE JEWELS

Once upon a time, in a deep forest, two princes lived in private kingdoms. In the darkness of the tall green trees, Prince Rupert guarded his riches — heaps of wonderful rubies. On the softness of the moss, beneath the yellowing poplars, Prince Esperad spread his wealth of shining emeralds. Each had his fortune to enjoy.

One day a traveller came to Deep Forest. She walked under the tall pines, past the coppery rocks, along the fresh cool creek. She heard a gentle singing. It was Prince Rupert, chanting as he laid his rubies on the bare grey rocks. Dazzled by their brightness, the traveller expressed her awe, then continued on her journey. She walked past the cliffs and the running river to Gleaming Pond. As she strode toward the poplars on the far side of the pond, she heard the tinkling of chimes. Prince Esperad and his musicians were admiring the emeralds. These too were things of great worth and beauty.

The traveller visited many lands and many peoples, but she never forgot Deep Forest and the jewels it held within. They were beautiful, but there was something missing. In the wider world, jewels of many colors could be found, and their dazzling beauty was all the greater because of the way the blues, reds, purples, and greens shone and shimmered together. If Esperad and Rupert could share their jewels, each would experience a still more wondrous beauty.

When the traveller returned to Deep Forest, the princes welcomed her warmly. Speaking in turn with the princes, she arranged for trade between them. She persuaded Rupert to give ten rubies for ten emeralds, and Esperad ten emeralds for the same number of rubies. "By these means," she explained to the solitary princes, "you will see such contrast of color and light as never before. You will gain far more than you lose. I will take from each of you a sealed bag containing the ten jewels. I will leave these bags at the Gleaming Pond. The emeralds will I place by the dark pines, for Prince Rupert, and the rubies by the yellow poplars, for Prince Esperad."

The day for the trade came near. Prince Rupert fingered his rubies, rubbing each in turn between his hands. "What is this wondrous combination of colors I am to see?" he asked himself. "It must be beautiful beyond what I can imagine, for the traveller has assured me this is so." Still, he lingered sadly over his rubies, trying to decide which ones he would put in the bag to give away.

Then an idea came to him. "The glowing colors will be mine to see, if I have the emeralds and my rubies, so the traveller says. To get emeralds I am to give rubies, but they go for the trade in a sealed bag. The bag will be left only for Prince Esperad, and when the time comes for it to be opened, his jewels will already be in my hands. I can get the emeralds without giving anything up."

This thought troubled Prince Rupert, but the thought of giving away ten of his precious jewels troubled him still more. He sat pensive in the dark forest night, thinking harder than he had ever thought before. Then he sealed an empty bag, locked his rubies in the family chest, and retired to his castle for an uneasy sleep.

Prince Esperad too was excited, but troubled. He wanted the new experience the traveller had promised. Still, he clung to his precious emeralds, not wanting to put even one in the bag for the unknown strange prince. Then a solution came to him. Surely he could get the rubies without giving the emeralds away. "Either Rupert will put rubies in his bag or he will not. If he does, I can get them without putting emeralds in my bag, and I'll have both my emeralds and ten of his rubies. If he does not, I won't have his rubies, even if I do give up my emeralds. Whatever Rupert does, I'll be better off to send an empty bag."

Prince Esperad explained the argument to his musicians, who could find no flaw and admired the princely logic. The empty bag was sealed for the trade and the court retired for a restless night.

The morn dawned bright as the happy traveller strode through the forest. By the dark pines she found the sealed bag of Prince Rupert and by the rich moss that of Prince Esperad. "How wonderful the colors will be," she thought to herself. "The solitary princes will see the dazzling beauty, and a new world of joy will open to them." The traveller felt happy and proud. Was it not she who had dreamed of the gleaming contrast of colors in dark forest and the trade that was to bring it about? Much else might come of this wondrous achievement.

The traveller knew that she would not return to Deep Forest for many years. Still, the prospect of greater beauty, art, and civilization for its peoples gave her a serene feeling of deep satisfaction. She placed the bags at the pond and smiled to herself as she strode away, thinking of the joys and beauties her arrangements could bring.

With anticipation, Prince Rupert rushed to Gleaming Pond. There was a sealed bag, just as he had been promised. He seized it and ran back to his castle. With a small knife, he pierced the seal. Such a vision the traveller had promised! He could hardly wait to see the emeralds with the radiant rubies.

But the bag was empty. Prince Esperad had given nothing, and nothing was there to receive.

Prince Esperad too was keen to see the rubies he was to obtain from the trade. He had told his musicians what was to come, and they shared his excitement. The whole court went eagerly to take the sealed bag.

All were shocked to find nothing within. No new world of experience was ahead. His marvellous argument had led only to this.

Life in Deep Forest went on. Each morning the birds sang brightly. In the afternoons the insects buzzed, and as the sun was setting, frogs and crickets chirped. The pines grew tall, the moss was rich, and bright flowers bloomed in the meadows. The rubies and emeralds, kept safe by the princes, shone as brilliantly as before.

But the princes were no longer content. Each felt something had been lost, something was missing. Each sat lonely, trying to think where he had gone wrong.

Prince Esperad's argument had seemed correct to all his musicians, the best minds in his kingdom. Yet it had led him nowhere. Long they labored with the mystery of it.

At last a young musician had an idea. "Sire," he said, "I think perhaps I am beginning to understand. You thought that only you would make that brilliant argument. This other prince, whom men call Rupert, he must be a thinker too. Perhaps he reasons, even as we do in our kingdom. Perhaps he too was led by princely logic to put a seal on an empty bag. We used logic to try to get the most for ourselves; he may have done the same."

"By jove," exclaimed Esperad. "Perhaps he's got it. I think he's got it. This man we know not may think even as we do ourselves."

"Something seems strange, Sire," the musician mused. "Your argument is perfectly cogent, as far as I can see, but it will work well for us only if other people do not reason in the same way. Is something not at fault? What is this logic which can lead us to correct decisions only when others do not reason in the same way? Should not the same logic work for all? Indeed, it is a profound mystery."

They decided to send Prince Rupert an official letter,

asking him to come to a meeting at the Gleaming Pond, bringing ten rubies for the trade.

Prince Rupert was sitting lonely in his castle when the bells clanged. His manservant rushed up the stairs with a rolled missive in hand. "Something new has come today, Milord," he said. "A strange man in yellow pants gave me this scroll. He says it is a message from the foreign prince, Esperad."

Rupert lifted his head from his hands to examine the missive. His voice strengthened and his eyes grew keen as he scanned the unfamiliar script. "This is a proposal for a meeting to trade jewels," he said. "Prince Esperad and two of his musicians will come to Gleaming Pond tomorrow at high noon, bringing ten of the emeralds. He asks that I bring ten rubies and come, with two of my servants, to meet them. We can see together the wondrous mixing of the colors, and then our trade of the jewels can be accomplished."

This was good news! The visions of contrasting jewels might still be his! Prince Rupert rang for his servants and advisors. "We have received a great proposal," he told them. "Our trade for emeralds will soon be possible again."

But the prince's advisors were anxious. Who was this Prince Esperad? No one knew him save the traveller, and she had long since departed from Deep Forest. Prince Esperad had promised to trade his emeralds for rubies, but had sent only an empty bag. Clearly, he was not a man of his word. The message proposed a meeting. But perhaps this unknown prince would send bandits to lay siege on the innocent Rupert. Perhaps he would come with false jewels, or violently seize the rubies and escape before the trade was complete.

"Sire, you must not go," they urged. "The risks are great, and hidden dangers lurk here. This man wants you to trust him enough for a meeting and trade. But he sent us an empty bag. He has shown that he is not a man to be trusted. We should not go to meet him, for great harm, even death, could befall us." Prince Rupert listened sadly. He was disappointed to hear these words but had to admit that the advice seemed to be correct. Prince Esperad had indeed deceived them before, sending the empty bag. A man who has once deceived can never entirely be trusted again, and one should not go forth into a deep forest to meet unknown persons one cannot trust. Rupert wanted the emeralds and the magic color vision but he did not want to sacrifice his safety or his fortune.

"I suppose you are correct," he replied sadly. With his sharp quill pen, he wrote on a piece of red-edged paper. "The meeting cannot come to pass. No trade between us will be possible. Rupert of the Pines."

"Take this to the Gleaming Pond," he told the servant. "With such people as this Esperad, we can make no trade." After the servant left, Prince Rupert sat pensive in his castle, thinking of the unknown Prince Esperad and his mysterious emeralds. What manner of man was this, who would first send an empty bag and then a message proposing a meeting? What would such a man think and feel?

Suddenly a thought struck him. Perhaps Prince Esperad had reasoned even as he himself. A terrible idea penetrated Rupert's midnight thoughts. "If such a man as this is not to be trusted, neither am I myself, for I too sent an empty bag to him."

In his troubled sleep, Rupert dreamed of the traveller. She said to him, "You, Rupert, are a good man. You are worthy of trust. Anyone can make one mistake. This Esperad is a man even as you. If you are worthy of trust, so too is he. Send another message, and agree to meet him at the pond."

When he awoke, Rupert felt happy and excited. He remembered his dream and the serene visage of the traveller. She had an absolutely convincing argument. He,

Rupert, was a man to be trusted, surely so, and this Esperad was a man such as he, a man who had made the same mistake as he. Therefore Esperad too was a man who could be trusted. The meeting and promised trade would occur after all. And how wonderful, to meet this Esperad himself after years of princely isolation!

Rupert rushed to the castle kitchen and gulped his hot porridge. Then he rang for his advisors and servants to tell them of his exciting new discovery.

"I am not sure, Milord," said his senior counsel. "For a dream only, should you risk your fortune and your safety?"

"Fool," replied the prince. "Yes, I was dreaming. But still, the argument seems right. There is no more reason to think Esperad evil than to think we are evil ourselves. Have the scribes send a message this morning."

But alas the message was too late. Esperad and his musicians were disappointed and angry about Rupert's response to their first proposal. "What manner of man is this?" they asked. "He sent no jewels to us, only an empty bag. He broke his promise to the traveller and to us. Then, when we tried to meet him to restore the trade, he rejected us, thinking us untrustworthy when we had done only what he did himself. To meet with such a man! We would risk much! Truly he deserves no response from us. We wish nothing to do with him."

And thus it came to pass that Rupert received no reply. He fell into melancholy and could not be cheered.

The princes stayed apart and never saw the vision of emeralds and rubies in the Deep Forest. When the traveller returned, she found that each had died a sad and lonely death. The jewels remained for their descendents to enjoy as they could.

The Game Of The
Golden Pieces

In the quiet of the evening, the tribespeople sat by the fire at the Gleaming Pond. While the flames flickered, the High Priestess told again the fable of the jewels. In days of old, two princes had been unable to trade jewels because each had believed he would profit best by seeking the most for himself. Each sent the other an empty bag.

Their day had been long and midnight was near, but the people never could hear the old tale without talking on.

"The princes were not well taught by their elders," said Asha, an old woman of the tribe. "Everyone must learn young to do unto others what they want done to themselves. If the princes had been rightly taught, according to this Golden Rule, the trade would have been possible."

"The Golden Rule is for innocents in the nursery," said Unuk, a tribal leader. "Of course the princes did not use it to resolve a question of trade. Rules of the nursery and home do not fit with affairs of state."

"That is not the answer," responded Ronum, a young huntsman. "The same reasoning must hold in all phases of our lives. Nowhere is the Golden Rule correct, for it tells us to give others what we want ourselves. People of wisdom know that different people want different things. Things go best when each seeks the best for himself. What the princes did was reasonable and proper."

"Reasonable and proper? Their loss was tragic!" Asha cried.

"Each pursuing the best for himself?" Onota demanded. "This is stupidity itself. Shall I apply your principle to my young children and my husband? No one would grow into man or woman if we all thought as you do, Ronum. The princes were led astray because they were selfish. They cared not for each other and could not learn to trust each other. Instead of the reason you defend, we need more love and trust."

"This is not clear thinking," said Dedek, a tribe elder. "Correct use of reason could never lead to error. The princes cannot have reasoned rightly. Each took too narrow a view of his situation, for he failed to understand that the other could reason just as he did himself."

"I think not," Onota insisted. "Their use of reason caused the problem, and to solve it they should have followed their feelings."

"The teachings of the gods would have shown them what was right."

"Had they no conscience? Did they not know that cheating was wrong?"

And so the talk went on deep into the forest night. The pond reflected the full white moon and the stars were bright above the pines. The High Priestess sat listening in silence. How great a spell this fable cast upon the people of Deep Forest! Yet had they learned its lessons? Did they truly understand?

"My people," she said, "your talk has been long. Tomorrow the sun rises early and all have many tasks to complete. We can tire, even of the Fable of the Jewels. Listen now, for I have a wondrous plan to set before you. It is a game that all can play and it will give us new thoughts about the fable and our life together. It is called the Game of the Golden Pieces, and it is designed for one hundred players. We have one hundred men and women in our tribe. At the end of the game, if you play rightly, you will all receive pieces of gold. The temple fortune will I yield for this prize."

Talk of the jewels and the princes ceased. A stillness came in the late night. Great was the amazement of the people, for never before had the High Priestess given them a game to play, nor the promise of such a fabulous reward.

"Where are you leading us?" said Ronum. "What is this Game of the Golden Pieces, and what must we do to play and win?"

"It is an easy and beautiful game," the High Priestess replied. "It is based on a simple combination of numbers. The dominating number, N, is calculated from a sum of two other numbers which you, my people, will make for me by your own choices. You choose to be Red or Green. To determine N, I multiply 3 times the number of Reds and add to it 10 times the number of Greens. You play the game by choosing to be Red or Green."

"But this means nothing," Onota cried, perplexity rising in her voice. "Red and Green are nothing to us. How should we choose between them?"

"There is yet more to tell. I will give away N golden pieces, but only if your choices are rightly made. You see, the Reds will share equally among them 2/3 of the coins, while the Greens share 1/3. The difference between being Red and being Green is that if there are coins to be given away, you will receive twice as many if you are Red as if you are Green."

"This is the silliest game I ever heard of," the young warrior, Taduk, said impatiently. "Everyone will obviously choose to be Red, and the game will be over. It will surely be very boring — at least until you give us our gold. Why do you call this a game at all?"

"It is not so simple as you suppose, my son. I have not told what you must do to win this game. At least 34 among you must be Green, or there will be no prize. Fully one third of our people must be willing to accept a smaller reward in order that you all may win. To win, this condition must be met. Otherwise you lose your chance for a fortune and a new life. Look how N is calculated. It is based on a sum of three times the number of Reds added to ten times the number of Greens."

"But your game is so unfair," Onota protested. "Greens are needed to make the number N great. Yet for their choice, they are rewarded less in the end. Without enough Greens, there is no prize at all, but when the gold is given out, they receive less than the Reds. Shouldn't Greens be rewarded for their unselfishness?"

"Then it wouldn't be unselfishness," Dedek said quietly.

"It is unfair."

"Such is life itself," Asha mumbled sadly.

"Is that how you understand my game?" the High Priestess asked gently. "Perhaps you are correct. But so be it. That is the Game of the Golden Pieces. You play by making your choices between the Red and Green so that I can determine the number N. To win, at least 34 among you must choose Green."

"This is a strange game indeed," said Dedek. "Are there rules about how we play? How do we decide whether to be Red or Green? And how do we communicate our choice to you?"

"You may talk to each other and reach agreements among yourself, working together to win, or you may make your choices alone. You will communicate your decisions to me in our Ceremony of the Secret Token. Those who have chosen Green may place a green pebble in my temple vase, and those who have chosen Red, a red one. None shall see another select the token and place it in the vase. In the darkness of the night I shall count the tokens in my temple. If you have won the game, the Festival of the Golden Pieces will begin at sunrise the next day. We will celebrate the beginning of a new age in our history, a brilliant new stage in the civilization we are building together."

"These rules are incomplete," Taduk said. "Supposing that we win the temple prize, how are you to know who is

Green and who Red? If there is to be a prize, all can claim to be Red, to receive a greater share."

"My son, you see deceit in the minds of others and you see greed as the cause of their deceitfulness. But the same reasons for tokening and for declaring Red and Green will apply. Once you have made your decision, keep to it. For the prize to be won, all must display a red or green circle on the upper arm, corresponding to their choice. Colors displayed must match in numbers my temple tokens, or there shall be no prize. To win, you must play rightly and honestly. Remember, at least 34 must choose to be Green."

"Still, I am puzzled," Dedek said. "These golden coins are to be divided between Reds and Greens, with 2/3 going to the Reds and 1/3 to the Greens. But what if all make the same choice?"

"If all choose Red, there is no prize. But if all choose Green, then of course you win, and N will be 1000, as there are 100 of you. With no Reds, Greens, that is, all of you, will receive all the coins, meaning that each man and woman will have ten golden coins to keep."

A hush fell over the group. Ten golden coins was a fortune indeed! With such wealth, many new plans and projects would be possible. Could these riches indeed be within their grasp?

"Now at last I think you understand the game. The hour is late and all must sleep to be strong for our labors on the morrow. As you work in the fields and in the kitchens, think of the game and your decisions to come. Talk much among yourselves, because great opportunities are before you. And do not forget the Fable of the Jewels."

Though all were tired, the night was not one for deep sleep. The people were too excited and anxious about the Game of the Golden Pieces and the difficult choices that lay ahead.

Early the next day, Asha passed Dedek on the way to the

meadow by the yellow poplars. "I think I can see the answer to our questions," he said. "We must play the game as a group. We must meet and decide together what to do. All should work for the good of all. I myself will propose that we all choose Green. That way we are sure of winning, and each will get the same share, a solid fortune of ten golden coins."

"My friend, your years have made you wise," Asha told him. "Let us call a meeting tonight. We can save much worry, and we can surely win if we decide together that all will make the same contribution and receive the same gain. Ten gold coins is a wonderful prize which is enough to make anyone happy."

At the meeting talk was loud and long. Dedek explained his solution to the Game. "We must all agree," he said. "We will play rightly if we all do the same thing. If only some are Green, then the Reds will receive more coins than the Greens, and there will not be the promised reward of ten golden coins for those who abide by the agreement. And if more than 2/3 of us secretly choose to be Red, there will be no prize at all."

"Surely you speak what is true," Asha added solemnly. "We must work together. Those who choose Red will make a small contribution, and yet receive a greater reward than the others. How would our tribe flourish in peace after such a thing had happened? Reds would have more wealth and power, and Greens would resent them for it."

"Friends, this must not be," Onota said. "Seeds of envy and discontent lie hidden in this game. We must play together or not at all. If there is even a single one who is Red, never again will we have trust and security in our tribe."

"What an exaggeration!" Taduk exclaimed. "Woman, have you no common sense? We have never all made equal contributions, and we get along well enough."

"Pure cooperation is simple-minded and unrealistic,"

Ronum insisted loudly. "You ask each one of us to make a choice that will give him less than he could have. If ninety-nine among us choose Green, and one chooses Red, that one will receive 662 gold pieces, while the many Greens will each receive not even four! Who would turn down such wealth? It would be stupid to give it up, and still more silly to think that everyone else would do it. Who will take for himself the risk of living in poverty beside wealthy and powerful neighbors? People seek what is best for themselves. Remember the Fable of the Jewels. The princes did not cooperate. Has human nature changed since then?"

"You have learned nothing," Asha said sadly. "Both princes were miserable because each started out caring only for himself, and then they came to distrust each other and could never recover from their first mistake. Selfishness isn't even good for the self. That's what the story teaches."

"The lesson of the Fable," Ronum replied hotly, "is that people will pursue their self-interest as they reasonably can."

"And lose in doing it!" Onota retorted. "Will you never learn? We must each make a rightful contribution and cooperate for the good of all. Then each can receive his rightful and fair reward."

The meeting lasted many hours. There was so much talk back and forth that when it ended no one understood what to do. It was left to Taduk to make the final statement.

"Men and women of Deep Forest," he said. "Dedek and Asha have explained why they think we should all choose to be Green, and how our tribe could benefit from such a strategy in the Game of the Golden Pieces. If we could enforce the same choice for all, we would need to vote here to determine what that choice would be. Perhaps then we would support Dedek's proposal. This I know not. But our tokening is secret, so the Priestess says. We cannot enforce a group decision. Anyone who wishes to follow Asha and

172

Dedek may do that, but each person's final choice is made only according to his own reason and his own conscience."

There were still several days before the Ceremony of the Secret Tokens. Everyone was preoccupied, excited, and worried about the great choices to come. There was much they could hope to win, but also much that could be lost.

In their anxious talk, the men and women of the forest worked out many solutions to the problem. Dedek's advice seemed correct to many, but all recalled Taduk's warning that a group strategy could not be enforced in the Ceremony. For all to follow Dedek's advice would be fair and sensible, and would yield a prize for each man and woman. But could anyone feel confident that all his fellow members of the tribe would choose as he did, if he chose Green? Such wealth and power a Red could have, especially if he were the only one!

In fact, many decided that Red was the rational choice.

It appeared that in almost any circumstances an individual would be better off Red, not Green. If a prize was to be given, a Red would receive twice as many coins as a Green. The chance that his own choice would make just that difference between there being 34 greens and 33 — not enough for the prize — seemed too small to be taken seriously. For these reasons, ten men and women chose Red.

A further stage of reasoning occurred to many others, who disputed the easy conclusion of these ten. "You think you need make no sacrifice," they said. "but unless 34 among us choose Green, there will be no prize. These simple arguments you give, for choosing Red, will occur to everyone else as well. Some must choose Green. Why not you? Are you so special that you have no obligation to make a contribution to the whole group? All must thrive, not just you. By ignoring the others, you will be worse off, even for yourself."

Then, hearing this argument and believing that many other men and women were following it, and had understood the need to choose Green, they thought a stage further. It would be all right to choose Red, for many others would understand the need to be Green and would make the necessary sacrifice. For such reasons, twelve more men and women chose Red.

But such was knowledge within the tribe that still further considerations entered many minds. Understanding the previous argument and fearing that many others among them would understand it too, they began to worry about losing the prize. If there were not at least 34 Greens, there would be no gold for anyone. Those such as Dedek and Asha, who had so strongly urged all to choose Green, would they act on their own advice? Surely they would. And too, many had listened carefully to what they said.

Still, it was hard to make the sacrifice. How could a

person tell how many of the others would token Green? In the meeting, many spoke as Dedek and Asha, and the gain of ten golden coins were great indeed. Were there enough people who would accept this, who would choose Green assuming that all the others would too? Perhaps. Perhaps not. "In any case, it will not be my own decision that will make the difference between 33 and 34 Greens. Whether we have enough Greens for the prize is something I can do nothing about." And so another ten chose Red.

To others, even these elaborate arguments did not go far enough. "We need to consider probabilities," they said. "And we should aim at a fair solution to the problem. The rational thing is a lottery of some kind. We need about 1/3 Greens. That would be 33 people out of 100, and there are the committed ones like Dedek who can be counted on to make up any slight shortfall which might occur by chance." So advanced was the tribe in its understanding of logic and probabilities that fully 48 people reached this stage of thinking. Each threw a die, designating to himself four faces which would permit a choice of Red and two which would demand a choice of Green.

None knew the results obtained by the others. In fact, 33 people were permitted to token Red, while 15 were required to token Green. But of these 15, only 11 carried through with the choice required. "It is mere superstition to base such an important choice on a throw of the die," they thought. "I cannot bear to make such a sacrifice for such a trivial reason."

Thus 37 more chose Red, while 11 chose Green.

There were other ways of making the decision too. Some had been affected by Dedek's simple approach and by Asha and Onota's support for it. They respected these wise older citizens, and reflected on their warning of the evils that might come from selfishness, great inequalities of wealth, envy, and suspicion. Five chose Green for these reasons.

Others worked out the problem by appealing to the Golden Rule. "I would want others to choose Green, so that as many golden coins as possible can be awarded," they thought. "What I want others to do for me, I myself should do for them. I should thus choose Green." Six people chose Green for this reason.

Still others remembered the teachings of the old philosopher, who had derived an entire moral code from pure universal reason. He had said that no principle of choice was right unless it could be willed to be universal. "Could I will that all should choose Red?" they asked themselves. "Obviously not. If all choose Red, there is no prize for anyone. Could I will that all choose Green? Of course, for then there will be 1000 golden coins to be divided equally among us. All will gain, and gain fairly. According to the teaching of our old philosopher, choosing Red is wrong and choosing Green is right. I am obliged to do what is right, and so I shall choose Green. So would say the gods themselves: act rightly, not just for yourself." For such reasons, five people chose Green.

Others sought help from the gods. There were no teachings about games in tradition, no rituals about tokens and gold. Still, was it not the Priestess herself who had set the problem before them? Clearly it was a problem for the soul and spirit. Long have religious elders taught that people should consider their fellows and conquer the base yearnings of the self. A truly pious man or woman should choose Green. For these reasons, four more members of the tribe chose Green.

So had the choices been made when the day for the Ceremony of the Secret Tokening was upon them. As the sun was setting, the High Priestess walked forth from the temple beside the Gleaming Pond. With her were two piles of shining stones for the tokening. But these were no pebbles! They were the jewels themselves — the rubies of Prince

Rupert and the emeralds of Prince Esperad.

"My people," the Priestess said. "Long had we known the Fable of the Jewels, but only now do I show to you the emeralds and rubies of the lost days. They are the treasures of our ancestors, whose descendents were among the founders of our tribe. While the jewels reflect the setting sun, let your thoughts reflect the insights we have learned from the ancient story. Play the game, make your choices, and enjoy the dazzling colors in the wondrous setting sun."

All gasped at the beauty of the brilliant emeralds and rubies. Honored indeed were the people, that the ancient treasures had been revealed to them as pieces in their own game.

And so the tokening came to pass. The High Priestess watched as each man and woman solemnly entered the temple with two of the precious jewels, one to be placed in the vase and the other in a chest beside it. The people of Deep Forest watched and waited in happy excitement. All talk was of the beauty of the jewels and the riches of the new age that was to come. When the last woman emerged, the sun had set. Dusk was upon them, and the Ceremony of the Secret Tokens was about to end.

"Retire to your homes, my people," the High Priestess said. "I shall count your tokens in the quiet of the temple. Tomorrow as the sun rises, return you here, for I shall tell you then what is the result of our Game of the Golden Pieces. Do not forget to make Green or Red in a circle on your upper arm, so I shall know how you have chosen."

All returned home and the night was quiet in the forest. But there was little rest. Anxiety and excitement kept the people from slumber. Greens were confident in their choices and hopeful that all had chosen as they did themselves. There was so much at stake! Had the people chosen rightly, to win the game? Would the gods guarantee enough cooperation for the prize? Would their people work together so all could share the new wealth?

Reds too were wakeful. Could others have seen through their reasoning? How would they react when they saw the red circle tomorrow? Would Reds be able to enjoy their fortune in peace? So much wealth and power was to come! A marvellous life was to be theirs, and it would all start tomorrow.

As the dawn approached, the people marked their arms and went to Gleaming Pond to meet the Priestess. They waited in hopeful anticipation, trying not to be too conspicuous as they stared at each other's arms to see the Red and Green circles. There seemed to be so many Reds! Could they lose the prize? But then there were Greens too, enough, surely, for the prize to be awarded.

The pink rays of the sunrise were fading over the Gleaming Pond when the Priestess came out from the temple. Her head was bowed and her hands empty. A cry of welcome rose up from the tribe. But the Priestess did not lift her head. Silence.

As people became uneasy, anxious murmurs arose among them. What had gone wrong? Was the promised fortune not to be theirs?

"My people, you have lost our Game," the High Priestess announced sadly. "From the Fable of the Jewels you have not yet learned the lessons of integrity and cooperation. We have only 31 Greens, with 69 Reds. There can be no prize. The temple fortune of gold will I guard herein, for a future time, for people of the future, who have learned to live and think aright. Go to your work and think again about the choices you made. Life can be only as before." She returned sadly to the temple.

Angry talk began among the people.

THE OVERHANGING CLOUD

The cloud hung low over the cities. It smelled of sulphur and fabrico-fost, and it was so thick that the people could not see the sun, moon, or stars. People lived and died, loved and fought, under the cloud. In the active centers of learning, clever men and women preserved and extended the teachings of the ages, while in the busy Parlace of Nations, where once the Gleaming Pond had shone, representatives of the hundred nations met to confront their many problems.

It was a dark spring morning when the two Sapiens from the Pluna Cumulogical Workgroup appeared to speak at the Parlace Emergency Session. The cumulists studied clouds — especially poisonous clouds. Most of all the Overhanging Cloud.

"Representatives," Sapien Nobel announced, "We have little time to lose. Our studies show quite conclusively that Cumulus 1016B2, commonly known as the Overhanging Cloud, is extremely near its saturation point and can hold little more fabrico-fost. At current fost rates, the cloud is expected to reach saturation point in three months. It will be able to hold no more liquid. At this stage, the poisons from the cloud will begin to fall upon us. Once the process has begun, it will not stop. Our old people and tiny children will die first, then the animals and plants, and finally all of us here on Pluna. The very waters will be poison. We must stop the use of fabricoes or we and our planet shall die."

"You must know," Sapien Stein stated, "that cutting back on fabrico use is not enough, not in the final analysis. All use must cease, or we are finished — if not in three months, then in six or twelve, or thereafter. According to our most expert calculations, which now have been checked by every member of the workgroup, Cumulus 1016B2 can hold 1.63T more fabrico-fost. At current rates, Pluna's nations excrete that amount in just over three months."

"We have warned you before, but our voices have not been heard. Now the situation is desperate. Something has to be done, and soon! Truly, disaster hangs near. Pass laws to ban the fabricoes. Men and women must learn to live without them, for with them, we shall no longer live."

"Remember our history," Nobel added sadly. "We had the tragedy of the Jewels, many centuries ago, then the Game of the Golden Pieces, followed by bitter wars. These stories are still remembered and studied by citizens of virtue. But they are light and trivial compared with what faces us now. Men and women lost beauty and wealth because they were too selfish and suspicious to work together. They had the capacity to consider others, to trust, to work for the good of all, and many could understand why they should do it. But too often they did not follow their own wisdom and conscience."

"They lost much, much indeed. Do we know better?" Stein interjected.

"We have to. Yes, they lost a great deal by their mistakes. Beauty and art, wealth and peace were sacrificed because people could not work together. But still, they had forests and meadows, clean streams and ponds, the sun, moon and stars. They had all Pluna's life to enjoy. Now so many of these glories are lost to us, and life itself is gravely threatened. We must know better than they, for our problems are far more drastic. Our civilization is an old one, stretching back through the time of the High Priestess even to Rupert and Esperad. If it is to endure, we must work together to eliminate these fabricoes."

Silence fell upon the Parlace. Faces looked grim in the darkness of the morning. All knew that the clouds were dangerous, and especially so the Overhanging Cloud, which cut off so much light and smelled so evil. Yet fabricoes had long provided the energy for artificial light. Those who were sickened by the smell had screens or masks. Life had gone on under the cloud for many years, and with considerable success. There had been predictions of disaster from cumulists and other pessimists, but few had believed life was actually so vulnerable as these alarmists would have it. It was only a cloud! Had a cloud ever killed anyone?

The fabricoes were the very foundation of the advanced civilization of Pluna. From rock, wood, soap, and water, they produced vast amounts of energy used for warmth, light, manufacture, leisure, and travel. In richer nations, every household had its own fabrico, while in the poorer ones, mass fabricoes served every village and city. Tens of thousands of Pluna's citizens worked with fabricoes in one way or another, mining rock, cutting forests, making soap, purifying water, manufacturing fabrico parts, selling, trading, or repairing fabricoes... Without them, life would not only be very different, it could scarcely be imagined. Many thousands would have no jobs. Fabricoes were the very foundation of the Pluna life-pattern. Yet according to these sapiens, they had to be eliminated.

Voices rose in alarm.

"Order, order, representatives. We must speak one at a time, or no one will be understood."

"We face great peril, citizens of Pluna. Listen to the cumulists. Long have they warned us and long been unheard. Now it is upon us—we must cooperate to eliminate these fabricoes, or we will all die in poisonous rains and vapors."

"Agreed, agreed. We are desperate. We must act to survive."

"For this emergency we call on all the learning of our ancestors. Green teachings of cooperation must be followed, or life itself will be sacrificed."

"Ban fabricoes now, or die. The Sapiens know what is coming, and we must listen and legislate immediately."

"We can pass a bill today, and each representative can take it to his nation. Nations must endorse that bill very soon, and changes can begin immediately. We must save ourselves. Death is not inevitable! Perhaps when there is no fost, winds will blow away the Cloud and we will even see the sun and moon again."

"Dreamer, dreamer. Your thoughts are in the past. The sun and moon have not been seen for generations."

" The sun is still out there. If it weren't warming us, we wouldn't be alive at all. We could see it some day, if the Cloud went away."

"Order, order, one at a time. Representatives, please."

"Representatives, representatives, is not our alarm premature? Fabricoes are the crux of our life-pattern. Who are these sapiens? Can they be believed? Are we merely to trust their word, when they appear before us to predict the end of life here on Pluna? How many cranks have prophesied the end of the world before? They've all been wrong."

"What are we to say to our governments and peoples? Any government seeking to ban fabricoes will be so unpopular it will be ousted from power. These Sapiens may be scientists but they aren't politicians. They know nothing of the real world. They are cumulists and cumulists only, men of the study, not men of affairs."

"An education campaign must begin. All across Pluna, we must teach the dangers of fabrico-fost. When the people understand, they will change their life-pattern willingly. For with poison rains, there will be no life and no life-pattern. Even the most elementary logic should convince people of that!"

"Logic, logic! This is an emergency!"

"Representatives, representatives, remain calm."

"Calm? Life itself may be ended, we may drown in poisoned waters, and you urge calm? You're crazy."

"Long have we told our people not to fear the Overhanging Cloud. They have been taught that life is rich and good and can go on. How now should they believe the cloud may kill, and life-patterns must change?"

The frantic debate continued. Nobel and Stein brought out models and maps, diagrams, and calculators. They sent for other members of the Pluna Cumulogical Workgroup, members from several of the many nations. Questions continued, and some representatives insulted the Sapiens.

But after many hours, nearly all were convinced. The Overhanging Cloud was near its saturation point. The banishment of fabricoes from the nations of Pluna would have to be a reality.

And so the Parlace was ready to act, ready to legislate to preserve life itself.

"We need unanimous consent to the Bill Against Poisons."

"Don't call it that. That's too negative, and we will never convince our people to support it. The right name is 'Bill for the Protection of Our Life'."

"No, be positive. This is 'the Bill to Bring Back the Sun'."

"Representatives, representatives. Stick to points of substance. We must work out the details of this important bill, and when that is done, we can give it a name. Do not speak unless you are addressing matters of substance."

The Sapiens gave the Moderator their proposal for a bill and debate went ahead in a more orderly fashion. No representative felt comfortable, for difficult tasks and trying changes surely lay ahead for all. To take this bill to a national government, to persuade that government of the emergency, to have the bill passed, to persuade all the peoples of Pluna that fabricoes must be destroyed...

Then, more than anything, to go on in life without fabricoes... Whence would come warmth and light? How would they travel? Scarcely any horses still lived. Could a hardy breed come from these few? The few bicycles remaining in the old object centers were ancient and rickety, unlikely to be reliable. In the learning centers, some studied old artifacts and technologies which might suggest alternatives to the fabricoes. But these were small efforts indeed in view of the problems the people of Pluna would face.

So much would have to change! So unpleasantly! And so soon! Truly it was a gloomy time, in a clouded world. But there was no choice. If they wanted to survive, they had to act.

Many hours passed. Toward evening the Moderator was about to call for the vote when an insistent voice broke through.

"Fellow representatives, we are ignoring the toughest part of the problem. Here in the Parlace of Nations we feel ourselves together, but we must recall that Pluna is made of one hundred nations. Fabrico use must cease, we say, for the Cloud is near saturation, as the Sapiens have shown us. But with only a little fost, life can still go on, and it can go on for quite some time. Sapiens Nobel and Stein calculate that 1.63T can still be absorbed, before the saturation point is reached. People may cheat, thinking they can do so without threatening life itself. Whole nations may cheat. What are we to do about this?"

"No one would cheat, risking life itself!"

"We must verify. Trust, but verify."

"Honorable Representatives, you do not understand. If people think others are obeying the new bill, they may come to believe that they could use a fabrico, just a little, in the dark of night or perhaps underground at night. Just a little use would not bring the Cloud to saturation. But such comfort on a cold dark night! People will be tempted, and if enough give in to temptation, we will reach saturation after all. It will just take a year or two instead of three months. Our legislation is flawed, greatly flawed. There's no point in doing anything now. It's too late."

"There is an emergency, a crisis. We must act quickly."

"Our nations and people will work together, because they have to."

"Not so, perhaps not so. Just a little cheating might seem to make sense. A person might think, 'If no one else cheats, I can cheat a little, because a little amount will not bring the Cloud to saturation. So that wouldn't matter. And if others cheat, we are going to reach saturation anyway, so I might as well enjoy myself along the way. Life will be so much better for me if I cheat a bit – I can have warmth and a little light underground, just a little.' Representatives, it is a real danger."

"If everyone thinks that way, we'll get to saturation soon enough."

"God knows, if some of us think that way we'll all be poisoned. Human nature is so corrupt! We are doomed."

"Doomed? Don't say that. We can't give up."

These were disturbing comments indeed. Even in the face of disaster itself, people might look out for themselves and their own comfort. They might try to preserve their beloved life pattern, thinking they could do it and make no real difference to the survival of the group. And if others thought the same way – why wouldn't they? – all would be lost.

"Representatives, we can guard against this problem. We have a Parlace, our Parlace police, national governments, national police. We are not a simple tribe. We can check for fabrico use and catch offenders. We will punish them severely, and make sure there is no incentive to cheat. If Greens had enforced their policy long ago, the Game of the Golden Pieces would have been won and the wars

185

avoided. We need not rely only on trust, because we have our governments, our laws, our police."

"Yes, all right, all right. I said all this to show the need for a second bill, a bill about surveying policing, verifying compliance, penalties for cheaters. We cannot rely on honesty and good faith alone, not when the very future of Pluna is at stake."

"Then let it be. Representatives, break for an hour, for cantee, and while you are out, the Parlace staff will draft a bill for verification and compliance."

The representatives left the Parlace and went out to the semi-darkness and the smog. A few lights flickered, but none could feel happy to see them. They could think only of the fabrico-power required, the fost excreted by the fabricoes, and the difficult changes that were to come. Still, it was a relief to walk about, away from the intense debate. The cantee was hot, purple, and strong, and revived the weary members.

"Can we escape this problem of trust? Can we verify everything, police everyone, deter every possible cheater?"

"Of course not, dolt. We still have to trust most people, because police can't be everywhere. But isn't it good enough? People do understand we have to change our life pattern. They have some sense, some conscience, some idea of their obligations to others and our planet as a whole. They have got to support this ban and really work for it. If they don't we'll be right back where we are now."

"Worse, even worse. Every little bit brings the poison rains closer."

"You can't say that having a lot of police means you don't have to trust, because if people really want to cheat, they can try to bribe the police. The system just can't work if the police aren't honest enough to refuse that kind of bribe."

"What if the police themselves want to cheat? Who will police the police?"

186

"Come on, we do trust people, we have governments and police now and we trust them and get along. If we didn't we'd have no history, no life. It's not so radical. Extend what we have. We can do it, to survive."

"Someone appoints the police, right? Whoever that is had better be honest and reliable. Suppose he wants to cheat, and he appoints some police who will let him do it? Then what?"

The cantee didn't taste so good any more. This was supposed to be a break, but the problems were everywhere. There was so much to do and there were so many ways things could go wrong when they tried to do it. So much was at stake! Not just colored jewels or pieces of gold, not just beauty or trade, equality, wealth, or pleasure. Their world itself, and all the life upon it.

"The changes have to come, and we have to work together to get them. We can't work together unless we believe in one another and make it work out. We've got to trust that enough people will follow these laws. We just have to."

"To work together we have to trust each other? Then we really *are* doomed!"

"We have to trust some people, somehow. Not perfectly, of course. There will be police and penalties. But these depend on people too. We have to be able to count on people to understand the crisis. God, that's not so much, is it? People don't want to die in poisoned water."

"Pray, pray to God. We can only ask divine help."

"I feel like giving up, just giving up. It's all so hopeless. Why not just enjoy the time we have left?"

"What kind of future is there for our children? We have to do it. We are strong enough, honest enough. We know what's right and wrong. We have trusted before, worked together before, and we can do it now too."

Voices rose in alarm. Of course there would be police,

security, punishments for cheaters. But the bill against fabricoes could not be perfectly enforced. There were risks that people would cheat, even that the police themselves would cheat. Yet the risks of going on with present life patterns and their high fost rates were greater still. How could they do it all? So much would be sacrificed by those who lived without fabricoes! Would it all be for nought? Who would make such sacrifices, not even knowing he could preserve life when he gave up so much? They had to believe they could work together, that enough would cooperate and few enough cheat. But how to believe it?

"Isn't it too late? Can we really do anything?"

"Maybe I can make the adjustments, do it. But what about the others? Some are bound to cheat, and we'll all just die anyway in the long run."

"Of course we can do it. We must have faith in each other."

"No matter what people do, we'll all die in the long run. So what? The point is for life itself to go on. Life."

"It's too late."

"It can't be too late. The Cloud isn't saturated yet. You know, they told us we can change and save ourselves, maybe see the sun and moon again. God, what is wrong with you?"

"I want to go off with my girl and get something out of the life I've got left. Can't we enjoy ourselves at least, in our last few months?"

The Cloud hung low, so low, and it smelled foul in the damp air of the early evening. There was just a little light, enough to see faint profiles and the outlines of the flowering yellow tripantheums. The fragrance of the blossoms was lost in the smoggy evening air. But they could still see blurs of the flowers and try to recall the bright and perfumed blossoms of days long ago.

"Look up. No, move, move quickly, get away from that bush!"

"What is it?"

"Something's coming down, there's a drop from the Cloud! My God, has it started already? They said three months!"

"We're going to die, we're all going to die. Where are my children? I want my children, I've got to get to them while there's still time."

"It's the poison rain, a huge drop, right on the yellow tripanth!"

There was a sizzle, then flames in the dark and evil smelling smoke from the bush.

"Where are those two Sapiens? Those idiots, why didn't they warn us earlier? One of us could have been burning instead of that bush!"

Stein and Nobel came running, to the shouts of the frantic Representatives. They put out the fire, at first ignoring the panicky accusations of the Representatives. In fact, the Sapiens, who that very morning had been using their knowledge to make other people start to worry, were less alarmed and shocked than the others now that an actual crisis was upon them.

"Look, we told you it was urgent. Now maybe you really believe it. Some of these drops have come down before, burning trees and bushes, even houses. They've been investigated, reported. But no one wanted to think a cloud could start a fire. No one would listen. It's urgent. We told you it was. Now *act*. Get in there and pass those bills and don't stand around here feeling sorry for yourselves. So, your beloved tripanth is gone. You can save the rest of the world if you'll *do* something."

In sober silence, the Representatives returned to the Parlace. The bills were passed. Each representative went to the nation he served, and each nation confirmed the bills, providing as many resources as it could for surveying and policing. Thus fabricoes were made illegal. All were to be

189

destroyed, a Fabrico Police was instituted immediately, and a twenty year jail term was imposed for violating the fabrico laws. Stein and Nobel and their fellow cumulists would monitor the cloud to keep an ongoing check on its saturation level.

Dramatic changes began on Pluna. Life was quiet in the evenings, for there was little light for reading and games. People padded themselves plump against the cold. Animals, especially horses, donkeys, and mules, were valued as never before. Small groups began construction of windmills, using diagrams from the old object centers. Keen to travel, they even dragged out old bicycles. From the dash-arounds, which had required fost, they retrieved the sturdy wheels for a kind of horse-pulled cart. Though it was dark and cold, slow and inconvenient, life did go on.

Still, there was obviously some cheating. Police forces were strengthened and people watched anxiously for cheaters. But how could you see what another was doing, in the blackness of the Pluna night? Some spoke furiously, urging that cheaters be executed.

Yet most people were beginning to feel optimistic, and even a little proud. They had accomplished much, and the fost rate was considerably down. Some windmills were already working, giving power for the manufactures of bicycles and carts, and warmer clothing. Music groups had formed to pass the hours of the darkened evenings. People were becoming accustomed to the changes. Some even thought the Cloud was a little lighter. Perhaps, even in their own lifetimes, they would see the sun again — perhaps even the moon and stars!

After six months, Stein and Nobel and their group of cumulists measured the increase. .2T. This was better than the .3T increase that had been registered after three months: progress had been made. Cheating had decreased by nearly a third. Still, all was not well, for there had been a .5T increase in total, and Stein and Nobel had warned that only 1.63T in all could be absorbed.

The Cloud seemed less thick. The air smelled better. Some people claimed to like the changes, saying life was more natural, they felt better and slept better. There was hope, mounting hope in Pluna. And then came the nine month measure. There had been .4T increase. Despite increased policing, despite the acclaimed success of the stringent laws and the growing comforts of their new life, cheating was on the increase!

Now there had been .9T increase in total, and only .73T remained as leeway! At the current rate of .4T in three months, less than six months of life would remain. Again, the saturation point seemed near. All these sacrifices, all this work, and they were nearly back at the beginning!

Again, the situation was urgent. Desperately urgent. Stein and Nobel collected all the Representatives to make a fervent appeal to all people of Pluna.

CHEATING THREATENS OUR LIFE.

CHEATER? YOU ARE THE ONE WHO WILL DESTROY OUR PLANET.

FABRICOES: DESTROY THEM, OR DESTROY OURSELVES.

The next measure was better: the increase was down to .15T, the lowest ever. People were adjusting and enjoying their new life. They did understand the need to cut out fost. The cloud seemed lighter and much less foul. A few optimists even claimed to have seen the sun, though it was hard to be sure, after so many sunless years. Things were all right. Weren't they all right?

But there was still danger. Since the passing of the Bills,

cheating had produced a total fost excretion of 1.05T in a year. This was far less than previously, and many sacrifices and changes had been made. But it still meant that only .58T more could be absorbed by the Cloud. They weren't safe yet.

The fifteen month measure was still lower — .13T. Wasn't this progress? Of course, of course, but still they had only .45T as room for error. Nine months, at that rate.

"These Sapiens, are they never satisfied? We do so much, we've given up so much. They don't stop complaining, all they do is harp at us and insist there is still a problem."

"To me the Cloud looks better. Haven't we done enough? How long can you have an emergency anyway?"

"Don't stop now. You can't. Look, .13T is low, but if we keep that up, in nine months we'll have only .06 leeway. The end will be very near. We all have to cooperate, we really do. We can't take chances."

CITIZENS. CHEATING MUST STOP, OR WE DIE.

WE HAVE DONE SO MUCH. HELP US DO MORE.

DO YOU CHEAT ON YOUR FABRICO? STOP OR WE DIE.

SACRIFICE FOR SURVIVAL. OTHERS SACRIFICED FOR YOU.

Can they learn in time? We must trust that we can.

NOTES AND FURTHER COMMENTS[*]

Can Computers Cheat?

The specific focus of this dialogue emerged from conversations with my daughter, Caroline Colijn, who, when twelve, claimed that her friend's computer had cheated in a game. Robin expresses some of the ideas Caroline had at that time, but her views on the matter have changed since then.

The Sperm, the Worm, and Free Will

The story about the sea urchin sperm is based on an account in the popular science magazine *Discover* (September, 1987). The science paper described originally appeared in *Cell*. As to the brains of worms, the article on Brains in the *World Book Encyclopedia* suggests that Robin, Chris, and Jan were right to agree that worms don't have brains complex enough for choices. It reports that earthworms have a very simple brain comprised of a large pair of ganglia in the head region. These "control the worm's behavior on the basis of information received from the sense organs." (Volume 2, p. 461.)

For basic information on hypnosis see the articles on "Experimental Hypnosis" and "History of Hypnosis" in Richard Gregory (ed.) *The Oxford Companion to the Mind* (Oxford: Oxford University Press, 1987). My information on the conflicting psychiatric testimony at the trial of John Hinckley, the young man who tried to assassinate Ronald Reagan in 1981, is taken from Brooke Noel Moore and Richard Parker, *Critical Thinking: Evaluating Claims And Arguments In Everyday Life* (Palo Alto, Ca.: Mayfield, 1986) p. 66.

[*]   A more comprehensive pamphlet of academic notes and comments is available free of charge to instructors of courses in philosophy.

God, the Devil, and the Perfect Pizza

The Ontological Argument has fascinated philosophers, logicians, and others for many centuries. It seems at once natural and obscure, at once hard to refute and obviously wrong. Few view it as cogent, but there is still not a consensus as to just what is wrong with it. Anselm expressed it this way:

> ...that than which a greater cannot be thought cannot exist in the understanding alone. For if it is actually in the understanding alone, it can be thought of as existing also in reality, and this is greater. Therefore, if that which a greater cannot be thought is in the understanding alone, this same thing than which a greater cannot be thought is that than which a greater can be thought. But obviously this is impossible. Without doubt, therefore, there exists, both in the understanding and in reality, something than which a greater cannot be thought. And thou art this being O Lord our God.
> (As translated from Latin into English by E.R. Fairweather; printed in P. Edwards and A. Pap, *A Modern Introduction To Philosophy*; p. 403.)

Robin's argument about the perfect pizza copies an ancient objection to the ontological argument: one posed in St. Anselm's own time by the monk Gaunilo. Gaunilo claimed that a parallel argument could be used to prove the existence of a perfect island, that this was absurd, and that it showed that something had to be wrong with Anselm's reasoning. Anselm replied by insisting that the idea of God was unique, for it is the very essence, or nature, of God to be perfect and to exist, whereas even if an island happened in fact to be perfect, no island would be perfect as the result of its very nature. Thus, according to Anselm, no island would have its essence and existence necessarily connected, as God does.

As to the Devil, it is really interesting to ask to what extent contemporary Christians really believe in the Devil as a spiritual being embodying evil, as opposed to some kind of metaphor for evil. Orthodox Catholicism is committed to the real existence of the Devil and other evil spirits as well; in fact, the exorcism of such spirits is still performed by the official church. Catholic intellectuals, however, seem somewhat embarrassed by such ideas. There is also variation among Protestant religions. In general, more liberal Protestant churches tend to regard talk of the devil as metaphorical, whereas fundamentalist Protestant churches remain committed to his or her existence.

My Brilliant Mathematical Career

The title of this piece is adapted from Miles Franklin, *My Brilliant Career*, written in 1901 when the author was only sixteen years old, and recently reissued (London: Virago Press, 1981). My own career in mathematics was moderately brilliant, but ended more than twenty five years ago – not quite in the way described here. My husband, Anton Colijn, has a Ph.D. in mathematics and advised in a number of the details in this piece. The story of the infinite hotel was told to him by a schoolteacher in Holland many years ago. I've also been helped by Rozsa Peter's *Playing With Infinity: Mathematical Explorations And Excursions* (New York: Dover, 1957) and by Douglas Hofstadter's *Gödel, Escher, Bach: The Eternal Golden Braid* (New York: Basic Books, 1977).

What Makes Selves?

The stories of Eve and Sybil may be found in Corbett H. Thigpen and Hervey M. Cleckley, *The Three Faces Of Eve* (New York: McGraw-Hill, 1957) and Flora Reta Schreiber, *Sybil* (New York: Warner, 1973). My psychologist friends tell me that present opinions about the existence of multiple selves in the same body are divided. *The Oxford Companion To The Mind* (see "Dissociated Personalities") expresses skepticism about the idea, saying that patients manifesting multiple personalities have tended to have doctors who believe in the idea and may be attempting to please and impress their doctors. Oliver Sacks' patients, Jimmy and William, are described in his wonderful book, *The Man Who Mistook His Wife For A Hat* (Old Tappan, N.J.: Summit Books, 1986).

Roommates In Space

The philosophical inspiration for this story comes from a debate in the 1920's between Arthur Eddington, a physicist and popularizer of science, and Susan Stebbing, a logician and philosopher. In one of his popular essays, Eddington referred to 'two tables', the ordinary solid table familiar to us in normal life, and the physicists' table, which isn't solid, but is mostly empty space because of all the emptiness between subatomic particles. See Arthur Eddington, *The Nature Of The Physical World* (New York: Macmillan, 1928) and Susan Stebbing, *Philosophy And*

The Physicists (London: Methuen, 1937). Eddington said the common sense picture of the world had been shown by modern physics to be false; Stebbing accused him of misusing language and analogies to give an overly dramatic and inaccurate picture of what physics was all about.

The eminent scientist Niels Bohr is reported to have said, "Anyone who is not shocked by quantum theory has not understood it." I've been assisted in my own efforts to understand quantum physics by many patient explanations by my husband, Anton Colijn, and by reading Paul Davies, *God And The New Physics* (Harmondsworth: Penguin, 1983), which is an unusually clear book on the topic. Davies reminds his readers that despite its theoretically exotic and peculiar nature, quantum physics is a practical, down-to-earth theory which "has given us the laser, the electron microscope, the transistor, the superconductor, and nuclear power." (He tactfully omits to mention the atomic bomb!) It used to be assumed that the atom would be like a scaled down version of the solar system, but instead, "the atomic world is full of murkiness and chaos."

Conscience

The characters in this dialogue express various fairly common arguments about the problem of moral judgement. I focus their discussion on conscience because of an experience I once had when teaching introductory ethics. I had found that people are so used to hearing that there is no real foundation for moral beliefs that students seldom reacted much to the idea. But when I once proposed that conscience was just a name for our awareness of whatever we believe morally, and its advice would vary for different people, one student was so shocked that he came to see me privately to tell me just how disturbing my views were. Alas, I no longer remember his name, but to him this dialogue is dedicated.

The Salman Rushdie case was a major international news story when these notes were being completed in March, 1989. Many moderate Muslims advocated censorship of Rushdie's book *The Satanic Verses* on the grounds that it was grossly insulting to their religion, but they did not join Ayatollah Khomeini in calling for Rushdie's assassination. Non-Muslims, especially writers, mostly took the view that, whatever the literary and historical merits of the book, it should be allowed to circulate as a matter of freedom of expression. A major demonstration of support for Rushdie and for freedom of speech was staged in New York by prominent American writers. Threats of violence were not limited to Rushdie himself, but were addressed as well to his publishers (Penguin in England and Viking in New York) and to a number of stores which carried the book.

A Sequence Of Events

These stories illustrate a problem which theorists call The Prisoner's Dilemma. Imagine two people who have jointly committed a crime, have been arrested, and are being held separately before their trial. Each is told that if he confesses, he will get a shorter sentence (say two years instead of five) in return for the evidence he can give against his accomplice. If he does not confess, then if his accomplice doesn't confess either, neither can be convicted and both will go free. But of course if he does not confess and the accomplice does, he'll get five years. The prisoners cannot communicate and they don't trust each other enough to cooperate. So they both confess, thinking this is the most logical thing to do. As a result, they both get two years in prison when they could have gone free.

These people act rationally in the narrow sense of rationality: that is, they each pursue their own self-interest. But, by doing so, they wind up worse off than they would be if they cooperated. The solution would be easy if they could communicate with each other, agree not to confess, and trust each other to abide by their agreement.

In some ways the Prisoner's Dilemma situation is not very realistic. For instance, people can often communicate about what they are going to do, and they often have acted cooperatively together before, so that they might have evidence about what sorts of things others would do. Also, they often need to interact again and again, so that not cooperating might seem to have costs which would be incurred in the future. One might reason "I had better cooperate now because if I don't, the next time I need his cooperation, I might not get it." The situation imagined for the classic Prisoner's Dilemma is a once-only problem, not a repeated one.

Nevertheless, the Prisoner's Dilemma has seemed to many people to reflect features of many real situations — from economic rivalry, pollution, and the population explosion, to the nuclear arms race. When people can communicate, they often nevertheless distrust each other to some extent — they may not believe what others tell them, or they may lack confidence that others will act according to their promises or contracts. Situations in which these dilemmas of self-interest versus cooperation arise repeatedly may be iterated, or repeated, Prisoner's Dilemmas. Robert Axelrod deals with them at length in his well-known book, *The Evolution Of Cooperation* (New York: Basic Books, 1984).

An especially clear explanation of the Prisoner's Dilemma and some important recent discussions of it, including Axelrod's, can be found in chapters 29-32 of Douglas Hofstadter's *Metamagical Theorems* (Basic Books, 1984). Hofstadter's first and simplest version of the Prisoner's Dilemma inspired my story of the princes. "The Game Of The Golden Pieces" was inspired by a version put forward by Anatol Rapaport on a videotape on conflict circulated by the Canadian disarmament group, Science For Peace.

The sequence of events depicted in my stories is not meant to express any commitment to a cynical view of human nature. Rather, the stories are meant to suggest that, in the final analysis, so-called rational self-interest is neither rational nor genuinely in our interest. To follow it will be counterproductive in the end. What is needed is cooperative action, and this, even in a context of vastly extended and improved institutions, will still presuppose some basic level of trust in other people.